WALT DISNEY

Genius of Entertainment

© Disney Enterprises, Inc.

Judith Pinkerton Josephson

Enslow Publishers, Inc.
40 Industrial Road
Box 398
Berkeley Heights, NJ 07922
USA

http://www.enslow.com

*To Walt Disney, who enriched my childhood and made it possible
for generations of children to feel wonder and joy.*

Acknowledgments

Thanks to Diane Disney Miller and Dave Miller at the Walt Disney
Family Museum for their insightful comments and help with this
manuscript. For her research assistance, thanks to my daughter, Kirsten
Josephson. For their encouragement and critique, thanks to Edith,
Donna, Karen, Connie, Jodie, Suzan, Marie, and Connie.

Library of Congress Cataloging-in-Publication Data

Josephson, Judith Pinkerton.
    Walt Disney : genius of entertainment / Judith Pinkerton Josephson.—1st ed.
      p. cm. — (People to know today)
    Includes bibliographical references and index.
    ISBN-10: 0-7660-2624-8
    1. Disney, Walt, 1901–1966—Juvenile literature. 2. Animators—United States—Biography—Juvenile
literature. I. Title: Genius of entertainment II. Title. III. Series.
    NC1766.U52D5439 2006
    791.43'092–dc22   2005036767

ISBN-13: 978-0-7660-2624-7

Printed in the United States of America

10 9 8 7 6 5 4 3 2

CONTENTS

1 Walt's Big Idea 5

2 Childhood & Farm Life 13

3 Newspaper Boy & Emerging Actor 21

4 Chasing His Dream in Chicago 30

5 Laugh-O-grams: A Good Hard Failure 39

6 Hello, Hollywood!. 49

7 Mickey Mouse Springs to Life!. 60

8 All the Colors of the Rainbow 70

9 Fantasy & War 81

10 "Zip-a-Dee-Doo-Dah!" 91

11 The Magic Kingdom. 98

12 End of an Era 105

Chronology 113

Disney Films & Television Shows: A Selected List. 116

Chapter Notes 117

Further Reading and Internet Addressses 125

Index. 126

Walt Disney

1
WALT'S BIG IDEA

As a young man, Walt Disney had told his father, Elias, "I'll make the name Disney famous around the world."[1] Years later, on the morning of July 17, 1955, Walt Disney, now fifty-three, looked out on his newest venture—Disneyland Park, a family amusement park in Anaheim, California. For months, Walt had been working toward this moment. At last, it was opening day.

From where he stood in his private apartment over-looking the grounds, he watched workers putting finishing touches on rides and walkways. He and many of his staff had been up all night. Outside the gates, long lines of people waited in the hot sun for the park to open.

Hollywood filmmaker and cartoonist Walt Disney had already created the world's most famous cartoon character—Mickey Mouse—along with other beloved characters. The company he headed, Walt Disney Productions, attracted some of the top artists, cartoonists, and story men in the country.

On his weekly television show, also called *Disneyland*, Walt, who liked everyone to call him by his first name, had kept viewers informed as to how the park was progressing. Sneak previews had sparked huge excitement and anticipation about Disneyland Park.

"I'll make the name Disney famous around the world."

Finally the gates opened. As the crowd of thirty thousand children and adults streamed into the park, tears of happiness filled Walt's eyes.[2] Nine-year-old Bonnie Williams would always remember seeing Walt that day: "He looked like a giant."[3]

Wearing Mickey Mouse ears, energetic assistants helped Walt greet visitors. Other employees dressed as Disney characters were on hand, too. People strolled down Main Street, U.S.A., an idealized small town much like Marceline, Missouri, Walt's boyhood home. From the Main Street hub, spokes branched off to other sections of the park—Tomorrowland, Frontierland, Fantasyland, and Adventureland. People marveled at the glittery, spinning colors on rides and the tantalizing scents of chocolate fudge and fresh popcorn. Their feet slowed to the clip-clop rhythm of horses pulling carriages.

Excited children raced into Disneyland Park on opening day.

Hollywood stars and entertainers of that time had received special invitations. Thousands of fake invitations added to the crowds. Other people had scrambled over the fence, entering the park illegally.

Walt wanted people to feel as if they had entered another world. And they had. But Disneyland Park's first visitors soon discovered that the planners and workers had run out of time. Only twenty-three of the park's attractions were ready. Those included Mr. Toad's Wild Ride, Peter Pan, Dumbo, Sleeping Beauty Castle, the penny arcade, and a miniature steam train that wound around the park.

> **Walt wanted people to feel as if they had entered another world.**

Due to a summer heat wave, the newly poured asphalt softened, and women's high heels sank into the walkways. There were not enough trash cans, drinking fountains, or completed restrooms, important features to Walt. The power went out in Fantasyland, and restaurants ran out of food.

In spite of these opening day problems, the parade down Main Street to the Town Square was a hit. Bands played parade songs like "The Stars & Stripes Forever." Walt rode in a car next to California's governor. Celebrities followed in fancy cars. With television viewers watching, Walt dedicated the park: "To all who come to this happy place, welcome. Disneyland is your land . . . dedicated to the ideals, the dreams, and the hard facts that have created America—with the hope that it will be a joy and inspiration to all the world."⁴

Linda Hopp was eleven when Disneyland Park opened: "Riding in the cars at the Autopia, spinning around in the tea cups at the Mad Tea Party, and seeing Walt Disney are still etched in my memory. . . . It was a day I will never forget."⁵

Four-year-old Ben Irick was thrilled to meet Donald Duck at the celebration in 2005.

Disney character © Disney Enterprises, Inc.

Disneyland Park's Golden Anniversary

In 2005, Disneyland Park celebrated its fiftieth anniversary, called the "Happiest Homecoming on Earth."⁶ Sleeping Beauty Castle got a pink paint job with gold trim and five gold crowns. Dumbo the Flying Elephant and other original attractions were coated in gold paint. The Main Street Opera House displayed people's memories of trips to the park. A Parade of Dreams moved down Main Street, U.S.A.; seven floats highlighted classic Disney stories, including *Pinocchio*, *The Little Mermaid*, and *The Lion King*. Each night a fireworks show called "Remember, Dreams Come True" played, and Peter Pan's Tinker Bell flew over the park.

Julie Andrews—the star of Disney movies *Mary Poppins* and *The Princess Diaries*—was at the park that day. "No matter how old you are or what language you speak," she said, "Disneyland is and always will be a place where imagination comes alive, the impossible seems real."⁷

To the children's delight, Walt Disney pretended to be a robber holding up the stagecoach.

Robert L. Waltz lost track of his younger brother in Frontierland: "We found my brother sitting in a stagecoach, enjoying ice cream with a Disney cast member," Robert said.[8]

"Right when we entered, I felt the magic," said author Connie Plantz, who was one of the children in the park that day. "There was a band playing Sousa marches in the town square, the sound of horses' hooves on cobble stone, and a general store where I could eavesdrop on someone else's conversation by picking up the receiver of an old-fashioned phone. Peter Pan, Mr. Toad's Wild Ride, and Snow White transported me into my favorite stories. Disneyland was (and is) a state of mind, a place where it is okay to make believe."[9]

> **"Right when we entered, I felt the magic."**

Once people entered this magical kingdom, everyone was a child again, regardless of age. One of Walt's friends described Disneyland Park as "the world's biggest toy . . . for the world's biggest boy."[10]

Baby Walt's parents and three brothers showered him with attention.

2
CHILDHOOD & FARM LIFE

When Flora Disney gave birth to a son in Chicago, Illinois, on December 5, 1901, she and her husband, Elias, named the baby Walter Elias Disney. Little Walt was content and sweet-natured. Delighted, Flora gave him lots of love and affection. The Disneys already had three older sons—Herbert, thirteen; Raymond, eleven; and Roy, eight. Roy willingly pushed the baby buggy along the sidewalk in front of the family's house. With his own money, he bought toys for his baby brother.

Flora and Elias had begun their married life in Florida, where she taught school and he grew oranges. When the family moved to Chicago, Elias started a construction business. Flora cared for the children and helped Elias with his business. Two years after Walter's birth, Elias and Flora finally had a baby girl, Ruth Flora.

But things were changing in Chicago. Many poor immigrants from other countries now lived in the Disneys' neighborhood. With their parents away working all day, the children of these new immigrants sometimes got into trouble. More and more saloons lined Chicago's crime-filled streets.

Elias worried about raising their five children in Chicago.[1] So in April 1906, the Disneys packed up their belongings and moved to Marceline in north-central Missouri. The family settled on a forty-five-acre farm. Its one-story white farmhouse had a wide front lawn, lots of trees, and two apple orchards with sweet-tasting apples. Here, Flora and Elias felt their children could grow in a safe environment.

Elias and his three older sons, now seventeen, fifteen, and thirteen, plowed fields and planted corn, wheat, and barley. He also bought milk cows, horses, chickens, pigs, and pigeons. Farm work lasted from dawn to dusk, with breaks for a big noon meal and a rest after lunch.

Flora cooked huge meals for her family, washed and mended shirts and coveralls, sewed quilts and clothes, and grew vegetables. She learned how to make sweet butter to trade for supplies. People said her butter was the sweetest in town.[2]

To four-year-old Walt, the farm was one big

exciting playground.[3] A dreamy, creative child, he was skinny with white-blond hair. He played in the mud under the bridge and waved to neighbors when they passed by. He helped his mother with chores, herding the pigs to spots where they could dig for grubs. The pigs even let him ride on their backs. Two-year-old Ruth was her brother's shadow. Everywhere Walt went, Ruth followed.

The changing seasons brought new farm activities, and the whole family pitched in. Elias and his older sons loaded a grain called sorghum into a "squeezer" that mashed the sorghum into pulp. Walt's job was to lead a plow horse tied to the squeezer round and round in a circle. The sweet sorghum pulp was later turned into molasses for pancakes, cakes, and gingerbread.

Each year at harvest time, neighboring families gathered to help each other with the big chores. The men and older boys worked in the fields or in

Marceline, Missouri

Walt Disney is Marceline's most well known former resident. Today, at the Walt Disney Elementary School, a glass case holds a desk similar to the one where Walt sketched and drew while in school. The town is the only place outside Disneyland Park that is authorized to fly the official Disneyland flag.[4]

Downtown Marceline, above, was used as the model for Main Street, U.S.A., in Disneyland Park.

the barnyards slaughtering pigs. The women worked in the kitchen. Smells of chicken frying and chocolate cake and cornbread baking drew the younger children there, too.

As Walt grew older, he and his brother Roy often rambled into the woods near the Disney farm. Walt loved animals and birds and soon learned all about forest creatures. When he did not have chores to do, Walt sometimes went fishing or swimming with a neighbor boy, Clem Flickinger. In the winter, they enjoyed going sledding and skating.

> **Walt loved animals and birds and soon learned all about forest creatures.**

Ruth did whatever Walt did, even if it meant getting into trouble. One day when their parents had gone to town, Walt, seven, suggested to five-year-old Ruth that they dip sticks into a barrel of sticky tar and paint pictures on one wall of the white house. When Ruth worried about whether the tar would come off, Walt confidently said it would. Walt drew houses with smoke coming out of the chimneys. Ruth drew zigzag lines. But when they tried to scrape away their artwork, they discovered that the tar had hardened. Their father was so mad that he left the tar on the wall for months.[5]

Another time, Walt staged the first Disney circus. He cut up some burlap bags and sewed them together to make a tent. Then he rounded up some farm cats

and invited his friends to attend the show. Everyone paid a dime to get in. But the farm cats would not perform. "You can't teach a cat much of anything," said Walt's friend Clem.[6] Walt's mother insisted that he give his friends their money back.

Relatives also visited. Aunt Margaret from Kansas City always brought crayons and pads of paper so Walt could draw. Grandma Disney had a mischievous streak and talked Walt into stealing turnips from a neighbor's farm.

Walt was old enough for school, but Flora Disney decided Walt and Ruth should start school at the same time. An avid reader and former schoolteacher, Flora taught the children how to read at home. In 1909, Walt was almost eight when he and Ruth entered brand-new Park School with two hundred other students.

Instead of listening to his teacher, Walt drew

Little Ruth happily joined her brother Walt in his many escapades.

© Disney Enterprises, Inc.

pictures of farm animals. Once he drew a portrait of his neighbor's horse, Rupert, and sold it for five cents. Walt was interested in many things, and his imagination was always working. But his poor grades showed his lack of enthusiasm for school.

What did get Walt's attention were the moving pictures that played on the big screen at the local movie house. If the movies were educational, his father let the children go to the theater.

Walt was interested in many things, but his poor grades showed his lack of enthusiasm for school.

Elias Disney was often serious and stern, especially with his children. If they misbehaved, he rapped them with a hickory stick. When he got mad, he used old-fashioned expressions, like "Great Scott! Land o' Goshen."[7]

Elias did not drink or smoke. But on Sundays he played his fiddle with friends and neighbors. During those music-making sessions, young Walt was surprised to see a different, more relaxed side of his father.[8] Well liked in Marceline, Elias was ambitious and a perfectionist, always eager to try something new and to do it well. In those ways, Walt was like his father.

Flora was different from her husband. Flora's sense of fun helped hold her family together. When nieces and cousins in the family visited, Flora got down on the floor and played games with all the children. Walt inherited his mother's sometimes-slapstick sense of humor and her warmth.[9]

The older Disney sons helped their father run the farm. Elias did not think the boys should spend any extra money they made on themselves. Instead, he thought they should help pay off the farm debt. Eventually, Elias quarreled with Herbert and Ray, who were then twenty and eighteen. Frustrated with their father, the boys secretly packed their bags and caught the late-night train for Chicago. They never returned to farming, but Flora later made Elias and their sons make up so they could be a family again.

After Herbert and Raymond left, the family struggled. Elias had only Roy to help with the farm work. The younger children sold apples door-to-door, and Flora sold her butter, but there just were not enough hands to

Walt got his ambition from his father, Elias, and his great sense of humor from his mother, Flora.

© Disney Enterprises, Inc.

do the farm work or enough money for the family. "If he [Walt] had a five-cent toy, that was a big deal," said Diane Disney Miller, Walt's daughter.[10]

Then Elias fell ill with typhoid fever and pneumonia. He recovered, but was never strong enough to do farm work again. In the fall of 1910, Elias and Flora decided to sell the farm and move to Kansas City.

The Disney family had lived on the farm for four years. But Walt never forgot those years. "More things of importance happened to me in Marceline than have happened since—or are likely to in the future," he later said.[11] He described the people there as tolerant, independent, and stubborn, traits that he shared as he grew into adulthood.

3

NEWSPAPER BOY & EMERGING ACTOR

Kansas City, Missouri, was big, noisy, and bustling with people—much more fast-paced than quiet, peaceful Marceline. Ten-story buildings filled the city's skyline. The Disneys' house at 2706 East Thirty-first Street was small and crowded. The backyard had just enough room for an outhouse—an outdoor toilet—and a small vegetable patch. From where the Disneys lived, nine-year-old Walt could see the buildings of Fairmont Park, partially hidden behind a fence. He heard the music of the carousel and the excited squeals of children on rides. But his father thought spending money on such activities was a waste of time.

Since Elias Disney's illness, he could not do heavy work anymore. So he bought a newspaper route. He expected Roy and Walt to deliver the papers each morning, evening, and on Sundays. The boys woke before dawn to collect the papers by 4:30 A.M. Roy and Walt then pushed the cart filled with newspapers down the dark street. On hot summer mornings, people called out their open windows to complain about the clattering and rumbling of the cart's iron wheels.

The boys had to place the papers on each doorstep, not throw them from the street. Sometimes Walt stopped briefly to play with toys left on people's porches—circus figures, toy cars and airplanes, or a miniature train. On winter days when it was bitterly cold, he liked delivering papers in apartment buildings. He would sit on the steps at the end of the heated halls and doze for a few minutes.

Since moving to Kansas City, Walt and his sister, Ruth, had attended Benton Grammar School. Even though his mother helped him with his homework, Walt was not a good student. Walt developed a reputation for snoozing in class, not following directions, and failing to hand in his homework.[1] He did visit the public library often, where he read books by Mark Twain, Robert Louis Stevenson, and Charles Dickens.

Walt liked to draw, and he had original ideas. When asked to draw a bowl of flowers in fourth grade, Walt drew people's faces for flowers, their arms for leaves. The teacher scolded him for not following directions. Walt doodled cartoon figures and pictures of mice in the margins of book pages. At home, he copied caricatures from the newspapers his father read. A caricature exaggerates a person's features, like ears, noses, or mouths. At the local barbershop, Walt drew caricatures of customers. The barber framed and hung them on the wall. After that, Walt's haircuts were free.

Walt started taking Saturday art lessons for children at the Fine Arts Institute in Kansas City. Elias "watched expenses like a hawk," said Walt, "but he would go for anything that was educational. He was determined to improve his sons, whether we liked it or not."[2]

Though Elias gave his sons small allowances, he did not pay them to deliver the newspapers. He told

When Walt took classes at the Fine Arts Institute in Kansas City, it was located in the YWCA building, above.

them food and shelter was pay enough. Walt dreamed up ways to earn extra money to buy things his father thought unnecessary, like cinnamon balls and movie tickets. Walt delivered prescriptions for a local drugstore and swept the floor of the candy store during his lunch hour. Some days Walt was so tired from all the hard work that he fell asleep in school.[3]

Playing sports with his friends lightened the drudgery. Neighbor Meyer Minda later talked about playing softball in the alley with Walt, though it did not happen very often. "Walt usually had other things to do. There wasn't too much monkey business about Walt," said Meyer.[4]

In the summer of 1912, Roy, nineteen, had graduated from high school. One day he announced that he was leaving. He had grown tired of not being paid for the work he did for his father. Walt did not want his brother to go. "Don't worry, kid," Roy told Walt. "Everything will be all right here."[5]

With all three of his older brothers away, ten-year-old Walt had to help his father even more. When Elias Disney remodeled their house, Walt worked alongside him. If Walt did not do things Elias's way, punishment followed. Flora Disney tried to defend Walt. "He's only a boy," she would tell her husband.[6]

Walt never complained. Instead, he did more things for fun. When the circus arrived in Kansas City, he followed the parade from beginning to end, with his younger sister, Ruth, running to keep up with him. Later he organized his own neighborhood circus parade by getting his friends to decorate their wagons.

He also retreated into his drawing. When Ruth was in bed with the measles, he entertained her. On page after page, he drew pictures of the same people in different poses. Then, holding the pages together, he flipped them fast like a deck of cards, so the figures appeared to be moving. Walt did not yet know the word "animation"—meaning to make figures move. But he had made his first moving picture show.

Walt had his mother's flair for humor. One day he came home with a gadget called a "plate-lifter." Squeezing a bulb connected to one plate made another plate jiggle up and down. His mother suggested they try it on Walt's father. That night at dinner, Flora squeezed the bulb. Sure enough, her husband's plate jumped up and down. Flora laughed and laughed. Elias said, "Flora, what is wrong with you? I've never seen you so silly."[7]

> **Walt did not yet know the word "animation," but he had made his first moving picture show.**

Another day, Walt's mother answered the front door to find a nicely dressed woman standing on the stoop. As they chatted, Flora noticed that the woman was wearing some of Flora's own clothes. Disguised in a wig and makeup, Walt had fooled his own mother.

When Walt was in fifth grade at Benton School, he memorized the Gettysburg Address, the speech given by President Abraham Lincoln in 1863 during the Civil War. Walt's costume included an old shawl, a cardboard stovepipe hat blackened with shoe polish, a fake beard, and a facial wart made from putty. His teacher, Miss Olsen, liked his performance so much that she called in the principal. The principal asked Walt to repeat it for the whole school. Walt had learned that he loved performing for people. "Miss Olsen always said I was going to be a real actor because I squinted my eyes on certain passages," said Walt.[8]

When the Disneys moved to a bigger house at 3028 Bellefontaine Street in Kansas City, Walt became good friends with a boy down the street named Walter Pfeiffer. Compared to the serious Disney family, the Pfeiffers were happy-go-lucky and fun. Walt Disney visited them often. Their daughter, Kitty, played the piano. Sometimes, the whole family gathered around to sing. Mr. Pfeiffer told jokes and loved the theater.

Walt and Walter started going to the theater to see vaudeville shows—short acts filled with slapstick humor, song-and-dance routines, and magic tricks. The two friends saw magicians escape from trunks and heard the latest hits of popular composer Irving Berlin. Walt did not tell his father about these theater visits.

The boys memorized the routines and jokes they heard and started performing them at school shows.

In one episode, which was called "Fun in the Photograph Gallery," Walt pretended he was a goofy photographer whose pretend camera squirted his classmates with water just before he took their picture. Then from his camera, he pulled a paper with a cartoon of the person that he had drawn earlier.

Both Walters liked British movie star Charlie Chaplin. When a local theater staged an amateur night, Walt and Walter created a skit called "Charlie Chaplin and the Count." Walt wore his father's trousers, domed black bowler hat, and shoes. He painted Charlie Chaplin's trademark mustache under his nose. Their skit won fourth prize. More skits followed. On nights when he and his friend performed, Walt sneaked out his bedroom window and hurried to where Walter was waiting. He thought his father would not approve.

One night, Walt's sister happened to be at an amateur night in town. An ad for the show had said that a man was going to juggle a stack of chairs with a boy perched on top. As the tension built during the act, Ruth craned her neck so she could see better.

Charlie Chaplin was one of Walt's favorite movie stars.

"He [Walt] was the boy sitting in the top chair of a three-chair juggling act," Ruth said later, "and I remember how very scared he looked."[9]

The world of entertainment dazzled Walt much more than the strict routine of school. In seventh grade, one kindly teacher, Daisy A. Beck, recognized Walt's talent and ingenuity. Walt was in her class for seventh-grade homeroom and for math. If he fell asleep, Miss Beck reasoned that he must need to rest. As coach of the track team, she urged Walt to join the team and learn how to sprint. He took her suggestion, and won a medal at the annual track meet. At 3 P.M. on Fridays, Miss Beck let Walt draw cartoons on the chalkboard and tell stories to his classmates.

During these years, Walt looked forward to times when Roy came home for visits. The brothers had remained close despite their eight-and-a-half-year age difference. Walt welcomed Roy's advice.

One day their father once again lost his temper with Walt, this time because his son did not hand him a tool. Elias yelled, and Walt probably yelled back. Immediately, Elias ordered Walt to the basement.

Roy was home at the time and overheard the argument. "Look kid, he's got no reason for hitting you. You're fourteen years old. Don't take it any more," Roy said.[10] Down in the basement, Elias grabbed hold of a leather strap.[11] But before he could hit his son, Walt snatched the strap out of his father's hand. When Elias then raised his bare hand to strike, Walt grabbed both his father's wrists and held them in place. Tears filled Elias's eyes as he realized that Walt was now stronger than he was. After that, Elias never again used physical force with Walt.[12]

Elias Disney did not like to spend money. But in 1916, when Walt was fifteen, his Christmas wish was for a pair of western-style high leather boots with metal toes and leather strips over the laces. Flora and Elias talked it over. On Christmas morning, Walt found the boots under the Christmas tree. He wore them every day after that.

The following spring, as Walt crossed the street, he kicked at a piece of late-winter ice with the toe of his boot. He screamed. A horseshoe nail frozen in the piece of ice had jammed into his big toe.

At the doctor's office, two men held Walt's legs still while the doctor pulled out the nail with pliers and gave the boy a tetanus shot. The doctor had nothing to give Walt for the pain. He used the few-weeks break from his paper route to think about his future. The Disney family had no money to send him to college. Walt loved performing, but entering the competitive world of vaudeville seemed impossible.

By the time Walt's foot healed, he had made a decision. Somehow, he would follow his heart and become a cartoonist.[13]

4
CHASING HIS DREAM
IN CHICAGO

A few months later, Walt's dream was given an unexpected boost. In the six years the Disneys had lived in Kansas City, Elias Disney had done well. But he had grown tired of the newspaper business and wanted to try something new.

For several years, he had been investing in the O'Zell Jelly Company in Chicago, Illinois. The company planned to make a new soft drink, a possible rival for the popular Coca-Cola. Elias sold the newspaper route and invested his profits in the company. He took a job as head of O'Zell's plant construction and maintenance.

When Walt graduated from Benton School in June 1917, he gave a patriotic speech at the graduation ceremony. Then he drew pictures as keepsakes in the class books of his fellow students. After graduation, Elias, Flora, and Ruth moved to Chicago.

Walt planned to join his parents in Chicago that fall, but for now, he and Roy stayed on in the family's home. Walt's oldest brother, Herbert, and his wife and young daughter also moved in.

Roy and Walt had very different personalities. Roy was good at math, studious, cautious, and smart. Walt was creative and imaginative, but also impulsive and careless. Patient and kind, Roy got used to finding chili stains on his ties after Walt had borrowed them. And Walt often pestered Roy to lend him money.

Roy suggested that Walt work that summer for the Santa Fe Railroad, selling newspapers, cold drinks, fruit, and candy to passengers. Called news butchers, these employees were supposed to be sixteen or older. Only fifteen and a half, Walt lied about his age, signed up, and got the job.

> **Walt was creative and imaginative, but also impulsive and careless.**

Wearing a snappy blue uniform with shiny brass buttons and a badge, Walt walked down the lurching aisles of the trains to sell his wares. During that summer, Walt learned some hard lessons. Sometimes the fruit rotted, attracting flies. If Walt could not re-sell the fruit to his customers, he lost the money he had spent. If he forgot to lock up his supply of snacks, some passengers helped themselves without paying.

In spite of all these problems, Walt remained

For Walt, working for the Santa Fe Railroad was exciting—and a valuable first experience in business.

spellbound by the excitement of trains and travel. He loved the plush velvet seats, the hustle-bustle of Union Station in Kansas City, and the lure of so many new places to see. Through the train windows, Walt watched the lush countryside speed by—dotted with town after town. At station stops, Walt talked with baggage men and other railroad workers. Sometimes the fireman and engineer let Walt ride along in the engine car that pulled the train down the track.

By the end of his summer as a news butcher, Walt had no money left over to show for all his hard work. In fact, he owed the train company money. But that summer, for the first time, he had felt independent. He liked the feeling.[1]

In the fall, Walt joined his parents and sister in Chicago. Though he probably found it hard to give up his newfound freedom, this huge, loud city pulsed with energy, excitement, and entertainment.

In an article about the freshman class at McKinley High School, one reporter for the *Voice* (the school magazine) wrote, "Walter Disney, one of the newcomers, has displayed unusual artistic talent, and has become a *Voice* cartoonist."[2]

Meanwhile, since 1914, two groups of European countries had been fighting World War I. The United States eventually joined the Allies, the group fighting Germany. In Walt's cartoons in the *Voice* he used patriotic, wartime slogans for his cartoon captions: "Help Uncle Sam Win This War," and "Buy War Saving Stamps—Save and Serve."[3]

Walt joined his family in Chicago, below, at the end of the summer.

Roy Disney had joined the U.S. Navy in Chicago. Walt admired the way Roy looked in his sailor's uniform and dreamed of enlisting, too.[4] But still fifteen, Walt was too young.

With his mind on the war, Walt could not concentrate on schoolwork. Only one other subject sparked his interest: cartooning. Three nights a week, he took classes at Chicago's Institute of Art. He learned human anatomy and studied with illustrators and cartoonists from top newspapers.

One of Walt's teachers drew a cartoon strip, "Tiny Tribune," for the *Chicago Daily Tribune.* Walt invented his own version, "The Tiny Voice," for his school's magazine. He scribbled down jokes from vaudeville shows to use in his cartoons. When Walt was not at school or studying cartoon making, he worked at the O'Zell Jelly Company, where Elias was plant manager. Walt kept the plant clean and ran machines that washed bottles and mashed apples. But he found the work boring and did not like the overly sweet smells of the jelly factory.[5]

The summer after his freshman year in high school in 1918, Walt, sixteen, applied for a job at the U.S. Post Office. Employees had to be eighteen. To look older, Walt borrowed his father's suit and hat and penciled a mustache onto his upper lip. Once again, he lied about his age and got the job. For twelve to fourteen hours a day, he sorted and delivered mail. The job carried a bonus for Walt—travel on Chicago's streetcars and elevated trains, which he rode free.

One day, his supervisor asked Walt if he knew how to drive a truck. Walt had driven a truck only once before, but he said yes.[6] With Walt behind the wheel, the postal truck sputtered and chugged through the maze of Chicago's streets. By the end of that day, Walt had taught himself how to drive.

Using a horse-drawn mail wagon, he also collected mail from Chicago's hotels. One particular horse knew every mailbox on the route. Walt set out, and the horse plodded along, stopping at each mailbox. When Walt came out of one hotel with the mail, the horse and wagon had disappeared. Walt ran up and down the street, peering around corners, but there was no sign of the rig. As he raced back to the hotel, he glanced down an alley that led to the next street. There, patiently waiting, stood the horse, with the wagon still hitched behind. Walt realized that the horse's routine at this hotel stop was to walk around the block and meet the mail carrier on the other side of the hotel.

With the money he made at the post office, Walt went on dates with classmates to see movies and vaudeville shows. He also bought a camera and tripod (a camera stand) and photographed himself doing imitations of actor Charlie Chaplin.

All that summer, people talked about war. Walt often heard a band marching along the street outside.

Recruiters followed, signing up men for the military. Walt's cartoon captions, "Your Summer Vacation—Work or Fight," reflected his patriotic daydreams.[7] Then one day, as he was about to go home, an explosion blew out windows and smashed bricks in the post office. Thirty people were wounded; four people died. Walt felt lucky to be alive and unhurt.[8]

People blamed German terrorists for the explosion. Walt wanted to enlist even more, but at sixteen, he was too young. A post office friend, Russell Maas, told Walt about the Red Cross Ambulance Corps, an all-volunteer organization that accepted seventeen-year-olds. Walt and his friend pretended to be brothers, listed their ages as seventeen, and signed up. Their lie caught up with them when their parents had to sign their passport documents.

Elias Disney refused, but Flora said, "I would rather sign this and know where he is than have him run off."[9] Flora signed her name and forged her husband's signature. She turned her back as Walt changed his birth date from 1901 to 1900.

At Red Cross Ambulance Corps headquarters, Walt and Russell got uniforms and settled into a tent. They learned how to repair ambulances and drive them over rough surfaces.

Right before Walt's group was to leave for France in the fall of 1918, he caught the dreaded Spanish influenza virus. This flu had already killed thousands of people. The 1918 flu epidemic eventually killed 40 million to 50 million people worldwide. In the United States, half a million people died. Flora Disney cared for Walt and later for his sister, Ruth. Then Flora also got the flu.

All three Disneys recovered. But by that time, Walt's ambulance group had already left for France. Instead, Walt was sent to Connecticut with another group of volunteers, including a young man named Ray Kroc. Later in his life, Kroc would found the McDonald's hamburger chain. Kroc described Walt Disney as "a strange duck." When the others went to

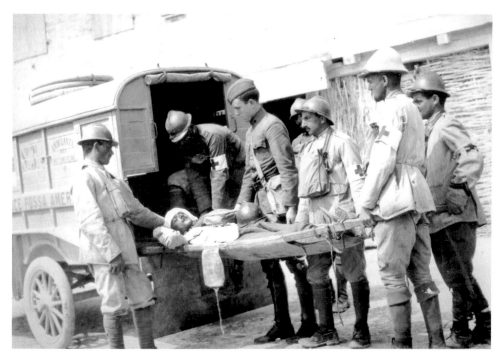

During World War I, Walt heard about the Red Cross Ambulance Corps, above, and signed up to drive an ambulance.

town to meet girls, Walt "stayed in the camp drawing pictures."[10]

On November 11, 1918, welcome news spread throughout Europe and America: Germany had surrendered. World War I was over. People celebrated worldwide. But to Walt, the end of the war was not good news. He had missed out on doing his part.[11]

One night the Red Cross announced that fifty men from Walt's unit would be sent to France to help with cleanup operations and with closing down military headquarters. Walt went to sleep, not expecting to be chosen. The next morning, his name was number fifty on the list. Soon Walt boarded a boat headed for France.

For almost a year, Walt drove military officers around, made deliveries, and did other tasks. Sometimes the food was bad, and his living conditions worse. But Walt did not care. He relished every new experience— sights, sounds, and meeting all kinds of people.

When he was not working, he drew cartoons, decorated the cloth sides of ambulances, and made funny drawings that other men sent home to their sweethearts. He met up with his friend Russell Maas. They had photos taken of themselves in their uniforms. They talked about one day floating a raft down the Mississippi River with their dogs.

For Walt, the year in France was exhilarating and fun. Now he was ready to go home.

5
LAUGH-O-GRAMS:
A GOOD HARD FAILURE

Walt had sprouted up and grown taller and more broad-shouldered during his time in France. But at eighteen, he still had his goofy sense of humor. As he told his mother about his experiences, he held out a box. Inside, to her horror, she found what looked like a bloody human thumb. Walt had stuck his own thumb (splashed with reddish iodine) through a hole in the bottom of the box.

After his experiences in France, Walt did not want to finish high school. His father offered him a job at the O'Zell Jelly Company for $25 a week—a large salary. But Walt said he wanted to do art and cartoons. Elias did not understand how his son could choose such an uncertain occupation over a steady job.

Against his father's advice, Walt moved back to the

Disney family home in Kansas City. Roy now worked as a bank teller there. The brothers reunited and shared their wartime experiences.

Walt took a sampling of his political cartoons to the *Kansas City Star* and *Kansas City Journal,* but these newspapers had no jobs for cartoonists.

Roy suggested that Walt talk with two local commercial artists, Louis Pesmen and Bill Rubin, who were looking for an apprentice. Walt's eagerness and enthusiasm impressed Pesmen and Rubin. They asked him to return with samples of his drawings. They wanted sketches of tractors. Instead, Walt showed them drawings of Paris streets. Walt knew nothing about advertising, but they hired him anyway at a salary of $50 a month.

Walt knew nothing about advertising, but they hired him anyway.

One of his first jobs was to draw ads for a company that sold chicken feed. Walt's sketches showed hens sitting on nests overflowing with eggs. Dollar signs floated overhead. Unlike many beginning artists, Walt welcomed suggestions. One day, as Walt was drawing sketches of cows licking blocks of salt, Pesmen—who was also an art teacher—stopped and corrected some of Walt's lines. Walt appreciated the help, and sometimes stayed at his drawing board for hours at a time.[1]

At Pesmen-Rubin, he made friends with another

eighteen-year-old, Ubbe Iwwerks, who later shortened his name to Ub Iwerks. Over the next six weeks, Walt and Ub created drawings for farm catalogs and Christmas ads for department stores. But after the holidays, both Walt and Ub were laid off. Walt found a job delivering mail for the post office until New Year's.

Walt's boyhood friend Walter Pfeiffer convinced his father to hire Walt and Ub to do lettering for the *United Leatherworkers Journal.* At the same time, the young men decided to start a side business. They called it Iwerks-Disney Commercial Artists. Iwerks would do the lettering and drawing. Disney would draw the cartoons and make sales to customers. Walt used $250 of his Red Cross money and bought desks, drawing boards, and art equipment. In their first month, Iwerks-Disney earned $135—an improvement over their previous salaries.

After the war, Disney began working as a commercial artist.

© Disney Enterprises, Inc.

In the spring of 1920, the Kansas City Film Ad Company offered Walt a job as a cartoonist for $40 a week. Walt and Ub agreed that Walt should take the job. Ub would run their business. But Ub was not as good a salesman as Walt, and the number of customers dwindled. Eventually, Iwerks-Disney went out of business, and Walt convinced his boss to hire Ub, too.

The company made animated black-and-white cartoon commercials for movie theaters. Though the characters' motions were stiff, the figures magically moved on the screen.

A cameraman explained the process to Walt. Paper cutouts of human and animal figures were pinned to a sheet. The figures on each sheet differed slightly. The sheets were flipped and photographed quickly (24 per second), creating the illusion that the figures were moving.

In New York City, Walt had seen animated cartoons, such as *Koko the Klown*. But those had looked more realistic. He and Ub bent the elbows and knees of the paper figures—showing the joints as creases. Walt pored over library books on animation. After careful study, he suggested ways the company could make their cartoons look more professional. Soon he and Ub were drawing the figures instead of making paper cutouts.

Unhappy with the jokes that copywriters wrote for his cartoons, Walt tried writing his own gags. For a bank ad cartoon, he drew a cow chasing a locomotive. Walt's caption read: "You'll never get anywhere until you get on the right savings track."[2] For a theater ad for a hat company, he drew cartoon faces instead of real faces under the hats. Walt was good at telling jokes and explaining his drawings.

He now could afford nicer clothes. Photos from this time show him wearing a tweed cap, dark suit, and tie. Handsome and almost six feet tall, Walt was popular with girls.

The summer of 1920 brought changes for the Disney family. In Chicago, the O'Zell Jelly Company went bankrupt. Elias lost his job and the money he had invested. Flora, Elias, and Ruth moved back to Kansas City. Elias looked for work as a carpenter, but he had limited success.

> **Walt was good at telling jokes and explaining his drawings.**

Eight people—Flora, Elias, Ruth, Roy, and Walt, along with Herbert and his wife and daughter—now shared the family home. When Flora made pancakes, her three sons had contests to see who could eat the most. Walt told his sister Ruth about his new ideas and plans.

Walt set up a studio for himself in the garage, paying his father $5 a month. All day, Walt worked at the ad company. At night, he experimented with incandescent lights, called "inkies," and drew. He borrowed a special camera and practiced making cartoons.

He soon sold three hundred feet of film—filled with short cartoon skits he called Laugh-O-grams—to the local Newman Theater Company. When Walt set the price at thirty cents a foot, he did not build in enough money to make a profit. But by then it was too late.

Everyday happenings gave Walt the subjects for his short cartoons, which theaters showed before the main feature films. Movies were silent then. Some movie-goers would read the subtitles—the words that ran along the bottom of the screen—out loud. This made other patrons angry. Walt created a Laugh-O-gram with a cartoon professor who solved the problem. The professor bonked the loudmouths on the heads or flipped open a trap door that offenders fell through, landing on the street. Former classmates from Benton School stopped Walt on the street to tell him they had seen and liked his Laugh-O-grams at the movie theater.

Roy wanted to marry a local girl, Edna Francis. But in the fall of 1920, he caught the flu, followed by a botched operation to remove his tonsils. Doctors diagnosed spots on his lungs as tuberculosis, a serious lung disease. Because it was contagious, Roy was sent away to a hospital in Santa Fe, New Mexico.

Around the same time, the post office transferred Herbert Disney to Portland, Oregon. Herbert convinced his parents to move there, too. When Walt said good-bye to his parents and Ruth at the train station, tears filled his eyes.[3] With his other brother, Ray, living in Canada, and the rest of the Disney family in Oregon, Walt was now alone.

Elias had sold the family home, so Walt moved to a room in a boardinghouse. He rented a small office for his cartooning activities and hired three boys to help him. He offered to teach them how to draw cartoons in exchange for their helping with his work.

To compete with the cartoons coming from New York's major studios, Walt hoped to lengthen his one-minute Laugh-O-grams. Filled with ideas, he planned cartoons built around fairy tales with gags and jokes sprinkled into the story lines. The first production Walt and his young helpers created was "Little Red Riding Hood."

He talked local businessmen into investing $15,000 in his very first company—Laugh-O-gram Films. Walt quit his job at Kansas City Film Ad. Soon Ub Iwerks joined him, along with five other animators and four staff people. The business relocated to a new building in a shopping center.

Filled with ideas, Walt planned cartoons built around fairy tales with gags and jokes sprinkled into the story lines.

Walt, twenty, was president of Laugh-O–grams, but he did not act like it. He did everything from running the camera to washing the celluloid sheets for reuse. Celluloid was a transparent material used in making animated films. Most of his employees were teenagers, willing to work long hours for low wages. Sometimes on Sundays Walt and the other workers met in the park to act out ideas for cartoons.

Using a $300 movie camera, Walt also roamed the streets of Kansas City, filming scenes for future films. Once in a while, New York newsreel companies asked

him to film special assignments. Newsreels summarizing the week's news were shown in theaters before the feature films.

Laugh-O-gram's big break happened when Walt made a deal with a New York distribution company, Pictorial Clubs, to make a series of fairy-tale cartoons, each seven minutes long. The company paid Walt a $100 deposit and promised

Disney decided to base his first short films on fairy tales, starting with "Little Red Riding Hood."

$11,000 more for the finished cartoons. Walt and his fellow artists had just finished the cartoons when word came that Pictorial Clubs had gone bankrupt. Instead of the $11,000 the company had promised, the only money Laugh-O-gram ever got was the $100 deposit.

One by one, Walt's employees quit. Ub Iwerks went back to work at Kansas City Film Ad. Walt moved out of his rented room and into the studio, where the rent had been paid in advance. For a time, the coffee shop downstairs let Walt eat meals on credit. Other times, he ate beans from a can. At night, he slept on a pile of canvases next to his drawing board.

A local dentist came to Walt's rescue in December 1922. He invited Walt to his house to discuss making a dental-health film. Walt said he could not come because his only pair of shoes was at the shoemaker's. He could not pick them up until he had the $1.50 repair fee. The dentist showed up at Walt's studio and offered him $500 to make the dental film. He also paid the cobbler for Walt's shoes and had them delivered.

Walt hired back some of his employees to make the short film *Tommy Tucker's Tooth*. Tommy Tucker was a boy who brushed his teeth, and Jimmy Jones was a boy who did not. "Nobody wanted to get anywhere near smelly, snaggledtoothed Jimmy," warned the film's narrator.[4]

Temporarily back on his feet, Walt brainstormed other ideas to keep his company going. One idea, called *Alice's Wonderland,* involved combining real films of child actors with animated cartoon characters. Walt worked on this film mostly by himself, using money borrowed from friends and his brother Roy.

Roy had been moved to a veteran's hospital in Los Angeles, California, where he could continue recovering from tuberculosis. Suspecting that Walt's money troubles would only get worse, Roy advised Walt to move from Kansas City to Los Angeles.

In July 1923, Walt decided to take Roy's advice. Walt went door-to-door, and parents paid him to photograph their children. "Then I went around to everybody I owed money to and told them I was going West to make a fresh start," said Walt.[5] He sold his camera and bought a one-way ticket to Los Angeles, California.

Walt boarded the train dressed in threadbare pants and a checkered sport coat. Inside his battered suitcase were a shirt, two pairs of undershorts and socks, drawing materials, and the unfinished film of *Alice's Wonderland.* But he rode west in a first-class seat.

Though his Laugh-O-grams company had failed, Walt felt positive about the future. "I was just free and happy . . . I was 21 years old going on 22 . . ."[6]

Years later, he said, "I think it's important to have a good hard failure when you're young."[7]

6
HELLO, HOLLYWOOD!

In Los Angeles, Walt gawked at the sprawling movie studios in Hollywood. Exotic movie sets looked like faraway places. Movie stars lived glamorous lives, had adoring fans, and made more money than most people could imagine.

Walt moved in with his sixty-two-year-old uncle, Robert Disney, who had recently come to California. Walt paid his uncle $5 a week for room and board. Like hundreds of other young people, Walt tried to find work as an actor or even as a director. He tried several studios. Each time the answer was no.

"Dad was a famous man long before I climbed out of my playpen," his daughter Diane wrote years later. "But he was Mister Nobody from Kansas City when he first landed in Hollywood, in July, 1923."[1]

When Walt told his brother, still at the Veterans Hospital in Los Angeles, about his unsuccessful job search, Roy said Walt should stick to cartooning. Walt had drive and self-confidence, but competing with older, more established cartoonists now seemed impossible.

"I was discouraged with animation," Walt remembered. "I figured I had gotten into it too late. I was through with the cartoon business."[2]

In fact not that much progress had been made in the cartoon field. Many of the most popular cartoons—*Katzenjammer Kids, Felix the Cat, Mutt and Jeff*—had weak plots and were little more than two-dimensional cartoon strips that moved.

> "I was **discouraged** with animation. . . . I was **through** with the cartoon **business.**"

Tired of job-hunting, Walt took Roy's advice and went back to working on *Alice's Wonderland.* In his uncle's garage, Walt set up a makeshift camera stand on orange crates. He convinced a New York distributor to give him a contract for six Alice Comedies for $1,500 each. They would feature a real girl, Virginia Davis, surrounded by cartoon characters. Virginia's father moved his family from Kansas City to Hollywood so his daughter could star in the comedies. Her salary was $100 a month.

Walt and Roy agreed to be business partners. Roy was finally well enough to leave the hospital. Walt would handle the ideas, the art, and the film side while Roy managed the money. To get the company started, Roy and Walt used $200 from Roy's military pension and borrowed $500 from their uncle Robert Disney and $2,500 from their parents.

Walt and Roy moved into a one-room apartment together, with a bathroom down the hall. Each owned one good outfit of clothing. At lunchtime, they often shared a single cafeteria meal.

Walt bought a used camera for $200. They rented a tiny studio and hired two assistants. After delivering their first cartoon, *Alice's Day at Sea,* to their New York distributor, they received a check for $1,500. With money from their second cartoon, *Alice Hunting in Africa,* they moved the business into a small store. The rent was $35 a month. The painted sign on the window read "Disney Brothers Studio."

People who saw the first *Alice* cartoons found them "nice and clean," according to the distributor, Margaret J. Winkler.[3] Critics said the cartoons needed more humor. Animation at this time was done completely by hand, not by machine. A single action could take as many as one hundred drawings to finish. Walt did most of the detail work himself until he talked his Laugh-O-gram partner Ub Iwerks into leaving Kansas City and joining him in Hollywood. A better animator than Walt, Ub began doing most of the time-consuming drawing. That left Walt more time to dream up the clever jokes and story lines for the cartoons.

Three women did inking and painting. They took animators' drawings and copied, or "inked," them onto the celluloid sheets. With paint, they added shading to each cel. Using a special camera, the cels were then photographed on top of painted backgrounds.

The first *Alice* cartoon ran in theaters in March 1924. By December, Disney's New York distributor, Charlie Mintz, had asked for eighteen more *Alice* cartoons at $1,800 each. Walt and Roy made a $400 down payment on a lot at 2719 Hyperion Avenue, where they planned to build a one-story studio.

One of the assistants Walt had hired to do the inking and painting was a pretty dark-haired woman with a warm smile, named Lillian Bounds. Shy and sweet-natured, she had just moved to Los Angeles from Lewiston, Idaho, to live with her married sister Hazel. Lillian's job paid $15 a week. After Roy and Walt bought a small truck to use for company errands, Walt started driving the ink and paint women home after work. He always dropped Lillian Bounds off last, eager to hear her stories about growing up in a small Idaho town as the youngest of ten children.

Several times, Lillian invited Walt for dinner with her sister and brother-in-law. He always said no. He wanted to meet her relatives impeccably dressed, not wearing his one ragged brown sweater and black-and-white-checkered pants.

The next time the Disney brothers received a check for an *Alice* cartoon, they celebrated by buying new suits. Right away, Walt asked Lillian if he could come visit her, and she said yes. After being introduced, Walt asked Lillian and her family what they thought of his new double-breasted, gray-green suit. "He just had no inhibitions," Lillian said. "The family liked him immediately."[4] She had grown up in a household filled with children, activity, laughter, and music. Walt and Lillian began attending the theater, meeting for tea, or eating meals with her sister, brother-in-law, and their seven-year-old daughter, Marjorie. When Walt was alone with Lilly, he shared his hopes, plans, and feelings. She was a good listener, and he liked that.[5]

As business partners and roommates, Roy and Walt spent a lot of time together. Inevitably, tension simmered between them. Still healing from his illness, Roy had been

> **When Walt was alone with Lilly, he shared his hopes, plans, and feelings.**

ordered by his doctor to leave work early and take afternoon naps. Roy did most of the cooking, and the food was plain—lots of "canned beans with lots of ketchup," Walt complained, making Roy mad.[6]

© Disney Enterprises, Inc.

Lillian Bounds came into Walt's life as an assistant in the studio, inking and painting the many cartoons needed to create a single animated action.

Love and marriage saved the day. Roy sent a telegram to his Kansas City sweetheart, Edna Francis, asking her to marry him. At their wedding on April 11, 1925, Walt was Roy's best man, and Lillian was the maid of honor.

Walt had once vowed that he would not marry until he had saved up $10,000. He did not wait that long. Soon after Roy's wedding, Walt asked Lillian to be his wife.

On July 13, 1925, Walt, twenty-three, and Lillian, twenty-six, got married at Lilly's brother's home in Lewiston, Idaho. Dressed in a lavender wedding dress and wearing a $75 diamond-and-sapphire ring, Lilly giggled nervously throughout the ceremony. On their honeymoon, the newlyweds stopped off in Portland, Oregon, so Lilly could meet Flora, Elias, Ruth, and Herbert and family.

"They were very warm and friendly . . . . ," Lilly said. "They loved him [Walt] very much and wanted him to be happy, so they were happy with me."[7]

Walt and Lilly moved into a tiny kitchenette apartment for $40 a month. Lilly got used to her husband working day and night. Sometimes after a night out with Roy and Edna, Walt would tell Lilly he had to stop by the studio to finish up something. Many nights, she fell asleep on the studio sofa as Walt worked into early morning.[8]

Every two weeks, Walt's growing staff churned out

two *Alice* cartoons, Roy kept careful track of the company's increasing expenses. Then the distributor of the films began making partial or late payments. Numerous angry letters and telegrams flew back and forth. Finally, an agreement was reached that protected the studio's rights and seemed fair—at the time. Disney would make all decisions about the content of the films, would share equally in the profits, and would own all trademarks and copyrights.[9]

In February 1926, the Disney brothers moved into their new white stucco building on Hyperion Avenue, close to downtown Los Angeles. A partition separated Roy's and Walt's offices, and there was plenty of open space for animators, inkers, and painters. Roy suggested that the company change its name to Walt Disney Studio—after the man at the center of its creative energy. Walt was determined to make this business a success.

Except for Roy, the production team members were all in their twenties. On a bet, Walt and several of the other men grew mustaches to look older. (Walt kept his mustache most of his life.)

The team worked long hours. To relieve tension, Walt encouraged everybody to take breaks, play baseball at lunch, and enjoy the beach. In spite of this, employees increasingly saw Walt as the boss, rather than as one of the team. Out of his hearing, they grumbled and complained about their jobs and the company.

After three years of making *Alice* cartoons, Walt was ready for something new. Universal Pictures wanted a new series starring a rabbit. Walt sketched plans for Oswald the Lucky Rabbit, his first all-cartoon film. The first Oswald cartoon, *Poor Papa*, made people laugh. Reviewers gave it positive marks. Walt added more animators to his staff and began creating a new Oswald the Lucky Rabbit cartoon every two weeks. For every cartoon, the studio received a check for $2,250. The mischievous rabbit had become a star.

Early in 1927, Walt and Roy bought vacant lots next to each other on Lyric Avenue. For $7,000 each, they built identical houses near the studio. Lilly's mother moved in with Walt and Lilly.

For Christmas 1927, Walt wanted to give Lilly a special gift. He knew she was not fond of dogs, so

Walt & Animals

Since childhood, Walt had loved animals. He constantly studied them. This later led Disney to make films such as *Bambi*, *Old Yeller*, and *The Incredible Journey*. He once said, "I respect nature and the creatures of nature. Man can learn a way of life from it . . ."[10] At home, he protected squirrels, gophers, and other small wild animals, even if they nibbled on his flowers or fruit trees. He considered animals "some of the most fascinating people I have ever met . . ."[11] Artist Salvador Dali said of Walt Disney: "It was the most natural thing in the world for him to imagine that mice and squirrels might have feelings just like his."[12]

he studied dog breeds until he found a type of dog that did not shed, smell, or have fleas. On Christmas Day, he handed Lilly a hatbox. When Lilly opened it, she squealed as a mass of fur wriggled into her lap. The chow puppy, named Sunnee, stayed.

On weekends, Walt and Lilly took road trips around Southern California in Walt's used Moon roadster, a popular touring car. Dark gray, it had steel wheels, a big hood with a light on the exposed radiator, and broad running boards that Lilly stepped on to climb inside. Walt liked convertibles, and the Moon had a canvas convertible top that folded down. In some towns, Walt ducked into movie theaters to watch his rivals' cartoons. Lilly stayed in the car with their dog. Later, Walt told Lilly what was good or bad about the cartoon.

In February 1928, Walt and Lilly traveled by train to New York to renew Walt's Oswald the Lucky Rabbit contract. The Disneys enjoyed a delicious dinner at the Hotel Astor with Charlie Mintz and his wife, Margaret J. Winkler.

> **In some towns, Walt ducked into movie theaters to watch his rivals' cartoons.**

But later, Charlie offered Walt less money per cartoon than he had been paying. Walt said no. Mintz said Universal Studios would keep the rights to the Oswald movies and produce them without

Disney. (Many years later, in 2006, Disney Studio got the rights back.)

Mintz had more disturbing news. All of Walt's key animators, except Ub Iwerks, had already agreed to work for Charlie Mintz. They were leaving Walt Disney Studio. Secret talks about money and working conditions had been going on for months.

What hurt Walt more than losing Oswald the Lucky Rabbit was losing his friends. He had hired his Kansas City co-workers and friends from the Laugh-O-gram days. Now he felt they had been disloyal to him.[13]

On the long train ride home, Walt had a brainstorm about a brand-new cartoon character—a playful, mischievous mouse. Walt told Lillian, "I'll call him Mortimer. Mortimer Mouse. I like that, don't you?"[14]

She did not. Mortimer became Mickey Mouse.

A Special Feeling for Mice

Walt Disney once trained a mouse to sit on his desk while he drew—"a mouse with a personality," he said.[15]

"Mice gathered in my wastebasket when I worked late at night. I lifted them out and kept them in little cages on my desk. One of them was particularly friendly. *I guess I do have a special feeling for mice.*"[16]

7

MICKEY MOUSE SPRINGS TO LIFE!

Back home, Walt shared his mouse idea with his best animator, Ub Iwerks. They brainstormed about how Mickey Mouse should look and act. All black except for his white face, he would have big mouse ears, skinny arms and legs, and a long tail. To make him look more human, they added big, puffy black shoes, bright red shorts with big buttons, and yellow gloves on his hands. Despite Mickey's colorful appearance, the first films would be in black and white, like most films at this time. The process and camera for making color film had not yet been invented. But as always, Walt was thinking ahead.

They decided Mickey should be smart, strong-willed, and positive, always looking on the bright side of things.

Mickey's personality sounded very much like that of twenty-six-year-old Walt.

"Mickey *is* Walt," said his brother Roy.[1]

A reporter later wrote, "Mr. Disney himself often notices that there was 'a lot of the Mouse in me.'"[2]

Disney animation historian Charles Solomon said, "Ub designed Mickey's physical appearance, but Walt gave him his soul."[3]

The story line for the first Mickey Mouse cartoon came from the news. In 1927, aviator Charles Lindbergh had made the first solo flight from New York City to Paris, France, in his airplane *The Spirit of St. Louis*. In the first cartoon, *Plane Crazy*, Mickey would zoom through the skies with his girlfriend, Minnie Mouse.

Walt wanted only those he trusted to know what he and Ub were doing. They talked out of the hearing distance of the animators who would be leaving the company for New York. Behind a locked door, Ub drew as fast as he could,

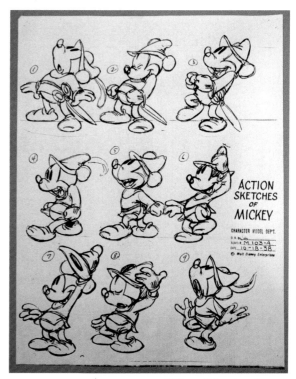

ACTION
SKETCHES
OF
MICKEY

An original sketch of a Walt Disney Mickey Mouse cartoon.

some days churning out seven hundred drawings. By the time *Plane Crazy* was finished, Ub had made eight thousand drawings. After work, Walt took Ub's drawings home to his garage studio. Lilly, her sister, and Roy's wife inked and painted. Later, Walt and another employee filmed during the night, stopping before people arrived for work in the morning.

A test theater audience saw *Plane Crazy* in May 1928. People liked it, but distributors told Walt: "Nobody ever heard of Mickey Mouse."[4]

Determined to change that, Walt and Ub and his small staff made a second cartoon called *The Gallopin' Gaucho*. This time there was no need for secrecy.

Up until recently, movies had been silent. Theater orchestras or organists had played background music

> **Movie distributors told Walt: "Nobody ever heard of Mickey Mouse."**

to go with the action on the screen. Subtitles told people what the actors were saying. Walt Disney knew that movies and film were on the brink of a big change: sound. It would be a regular part of the movie itself, the way it is in movies today.

Walt boldly announced that the third Mickey Mouse cartoon, called *Steamboat Willie*, would feature sound and music. Like many other filmmakers, Walt had no sound equipment in his studio. Walt, Ub, and young staff member Wilfred Jackson marked the film to show where music and sound effects could go.

"I bought a blank pad of bar-music sheets," said Walt. "I'd ask Jackson to play a tune on his harmonica, and we'd lay out our drawings so we had the right ratio of drawings to each bar of music."[5]

One night, they invited their wives to a private screening. Roy Disney ran the projector. The other men stood behind the screen and added sound effects with cowbells, a washboard, slide whistle, tin cans, a toilet plunger, and other noisemaking gadgets. The sound effects did not quite match the scenes, but sound came out of everything—cows, pigs, the steamboat whistle. Walt and Ub were excited about this wonderful new possibility for their cartoons and the Disney Studio.[6]

In September 1928 Walt headed for New York, armed with a musical score written by his friend Carl Stalling to match the film. The music included a vaudeville tune, "Steamboat Bill" and a country jig, "Turkey in the Straw."

In New York City, Walt found he was not the only moviemaker scrambling to add sound effects, talking, and music to their films. A few weeks later, Walt met Pat Powers, who owned his own sound system,

Talkies

In 1927, Warner Brothers released the film *The Jazz Singer*. To the surprise of moviegoers used to silent films, when Al Jolsen opened his mouth, people heard his booming voice. *The Jazz Singer* was the first film in which the audience heard the actors sing and talk. Many more movies with sound followed. After that, sound movies were called "talkies."

Cinephone. He promised to help Walt find a company to release the film. Powers impressed Walt, who immediately trusted the smooth-talking older man.

Powers arranged for thirty musicians and four sound-effects people to gather in a recording studio. Walt provided the high, squeaky voice of Mickey, along with Minnie's voice, and a parrot squawking, "Man overboard!" The first recording session did not go well. Walt paid Powers more money for a second recording session.

Finally, Walt had a sound cartoon of *Steamboat Willie* to take to film distributors. They liked it, but nobody offered to buy and promote it.

Walt wrote frequent letters and sent telegrams to people back home. He told Lilly that New York was beginning to make him nervous and give him the "heebie jeebies."[7]

Meanwhile in Los Angeles, Ub Iwerks was drawing the fourth Mickey Mouse cartoon, *Barn Dance*. Each cartoon cost $2,500. To pay for Walt's recording efforts in New York City, Roy had to sell Walt's car— his beloved Moon roadster.

Just when Mickey Mouse seemed doomed to failure, a man named Harry Reichenbach offered to pay Walt $1,000 to show *Steamboat Willie* for two weeks in his New York movie theater. The cartoon first ran on November 18, 1928. Within days, crowds flocked to the theater—drawn by *Steamboat Willie*, not by the feature film. One magazine writer said that the sound "hopped, it jangled, it twitched, it plankety-planked, and from that day forward was known as 'Mickey-Mouse Music.'"[8]

Mickey Mouse had become a smash hit. Movie theater chains and Hollywood studios now clamored for Walt's attention. He stayed loyal to Pat Powers, whose sound equipment had made *Steamboat Willie* possible. Powers promised to give Walt and Roy all but 10 percent of the profit on Mickey Mouse cartoons. Walt hurriedly skimmed the contract and signed it. Later, when Roy read it more carefully, he objected to several parts, including the studio's having to pay $26,000 a year for ten years to use Powers's equipment. Convinced that Powers was honest, Walt brushed off Roy's concerns.

> **Within days, crowds flocked to the theater. Mickey Mouse had become a smash hit.**

In the next few months, Walt added sound to all the Mickey Mouse films. Before long, Mickey Mouse was an international star. In Germany, he was Micky Maus; in Japan, Miki Kuchi; and in Spanish-speaking countries, Miguel Ratoncito.[9] Magazine writers wanted articles about this fun-loving, boyish mouse.

Walt did the Mouse's talking, describing him as a "shy little feller. . . . He's never been the type that

Before long, Mickey Mouse was a major movie star.

would go in for swimming pools and night clubs; more the simple country boy at heart. Lives on a quiet residential street, has occasional dates with his girlfriend, Minnie, doesn't drink or smoke, likes the movies and band concerts."[10]

Walt also favored a good night's sleep over Hollywood's nightlife, and he was devoted to Lillian. "Mickey would be lost without his Minnie," one reporter wrote. "So would Walt [without Lillian]."[11] Walt provided Mickey Mouse's voice until 1947.

By 1929, Walt and Ub had begun the Silly Symphonies series—humorous stories built around familiar musical themes. In the first, called *The Skeleton Dance*, skeletons rose from their graves at midnight and cavorted to mysterious-sounding music. Carl Stalling, now an in-house Disney composer, wrote the music, weaving in themes from Norwegian composer Edvard Grieg.[12] The idea of skeletons dancing seemed sinister to some people; others loved it.

Roy Disney had noted that Pat Powers sent payments late. When he did make them, they were much less than expected. Roy decided to talk in person with Powers. In New York, Powers did not give Roy the accounting information he needed. Powers also called *The Skeleton Dance* "gruesome" and said, "They don't want this stuff. More mice."[13]

Roy eventually discovered that Powers owed the Walt Disney Studio $150,000 from the Mickey films.

The studio broke off its agreement with Pat Powers and paid him $50,000 to get the copyrights back for the Mickey Mouse films. Copyright means that an author, composer, or other creative person owns the right to publish or distribute his or her original work. Walt eventually struck a deal with Columbia Pictures to distribute some, but not all, of the Disney cartoons.

Ub Iwerks and Walt Disney had been friends since the early Kansas City years. The two had always had contrasting personalities. Walt was brash and bold, self-confident, and a risk-taker. Ub was gentle and shy, but a gifted artist and animator, and extremely talented at technical and mechanical things. Ub had brought to life countless ideas hatched during their idea and story-board sessions. But lately, their relationship had grown tense. To keep up with the demand for Mickey Mouse films, Ub had been working overtime. In early 1930, Walt got shocking news: Ub Iwerks was leaving Walt Disney Studio to form his own animation company. Both Walt and the studio felt the loss.

1929 Stock Market Crash

On October 29, 1929, known as Black Tuesday, the U.S. stock market crashed. Shares of stock in U.S. companies lost most of their value. In the Great Depression that followed, banks and businesses failed, and many people lost their jobs, life savings, and homes. America's financial situation did not improve until the mid-1930s and early 1940s. In spite of this, people kept going to the movies. For just pennies, people could watch cartoons and movies that allowed them to escape reality. This helped Walt Disney and other studios stay afloat.

For some time, Walt and Lilly had been hoping to start a family, but Lilly had had two miscarriages. Walt loved kids and once told his sister Ruth that he wanted ten children, and he would let them do whatever they wanted.[14] At Christmastime, nieces, nephews, and children of close friends received gifts from Walt. Worried that he and Lilly would not be able to have children of their own, Walt threw himself even more into his work, becoming irritable and demanding.[15]

In 1931 when Walt was almost thirty, he had a nervous breakdown. Doctors ordered Walt to take some time off and get more exercise. Walt and Lilly took a cruise and a long vacation, and Walt came home refreshed. He started playing golf, badminton, and polo. He bought several polo ponies, and hired a polo coach to teach him and his staff how to play the game, including Roy.[16]

Mickey Mouse was now so popular that even the president of the United States, Franklin Delano Roosevelt, was a fan. The Disney brothers licensed the sale of quality Disney products. Soon Mickey and Minnie Mouse began appearing on alarm clocks, wristwatches, as dolls, and many other items. The money that flowed in helped Roy Disney pay off outstanding debts.

But Walt's mind was already on the next film frontier.

8
ALL THE COLORS OF THE RAINBOW

"I want color," Walt told Roy, sensing the next big change in the cartoon industry.[1] Until then, color choices had been limited; the results were often blurry and dull. A new company, Technicolor, had developed a way to make clear, bright colors. Walt signed a contract with Technicolor. The company agreed to let Disney have exclusive use of their technique for two years.

One of the first films Disney made after that was *Flowers and Trees*. It used Technicolor's three-color process, which could produce all the colors of the rainbow. *Flowers and Trees* was a love story about two trees. The cartoon won a 1932 Academy Award, the first in a new category for Short Subject: Cartoon. A special honorary award also went to Walt Disney for the creation of Mickey Mouse.

The studio's next Silly Symphony cartoon was *Three Little Pigs*, which a reviewer described as the story of "a big, bad wolf pursuing three little pigs building houses . . . made to withstand the huffing and puffing of the wicked wolf."[2] The movie's catchy defiant song "Who's Afraid of the Big Bad Wolf?" used "simplicity and repetition of a single line," according to a reporter, "and these two things point to Disney's climb to success in the cartoon field."[3] Theaters often gave the movie top billing on the marquee over the main feature.

United Artists wanted more pig cartoons. Walt

Coaxing a penguin to perform is not easy. Here, Disney was working on a Silly Symphony called *Peculiar Penguins*.

usually avoided repeating themes or story lines, but he did three more. None became as popular as the first one. "You can't top pigs with pigs," he said.[4]

In early 1933, Lilly learned that she was pregnant again. Twice before, she had miscarried. This time, everything seemed fine. The Disneys' extra bedroom rapidly filled up with furniture and "all kinds of pink and blue 'tinies' that I don't know anything about," Walt wrote to his mother.[5]

At a *Parents* magazine ceremony honoring Walt, thirty-two, on December 18, 1933, someone handed him a note. He read it, raced out of the room, and rushed to the hospital just before Lilly gave birth to a daughter, Diane Marie Disney.

Walt and Lilly built a new home close to the studio. It had a swimming pool, large living room, and a beautiful nursery on the top floor. In 1934, the Disneys' Christmas tree was as tall as their two-story living room. Scattered underneath were all kinds of toys for one-year-old Diane.

By 1934, Walt Disney Studio had grown to a staff of close to two hundred people. Walt insisted that all employees call him "Walt," just as friends and people outside the studio did. Only the studio carpenter called him "Mr. Disney," so Walt called the older man "Mr. Rogers."[6] Decades later, Walt's secretary Lucille Martin called Walt "Sir," until he gave her a cartoon that read, "Down with Sir!"[7]

At every level of cartoon making, Walt suggested ways to improve story lines and jokes. "Walt puts up his mild front . . . but underneath it there's drive, drive, drive," Roy Disney said.[8]

Walt hired the best people possible, and said, "their ability shows in the pictures."[9] He thought of animators as the studio's master builders. Whatever his studio produced had to be better than anyone else's.[10]

Competitors tried going behind Walt's back. "Let Disney win the awards and train the artists," said one. "I'll hire them away from him and make the money."[11] But other companies' cartoons were not as clever and unusual as Disney's were.[12]

Walt's personal habits were well known among his staff.[13] He was meticulous about his clothes, and he never left the house for an important event without looking neat and dapper. At work or at home, he favored shirts open at the neck, sweaters, scuffed

Making Better Cartoons

"A lot of people in my business were getting by on what I call a bag of tricks," said Walt, "so I decided to step out of their class by setting up my own training school. . . . I wanted to improve our backgrounds and improve our animation, and I wanted to set up an 'effects' department, so we could learn how to make a raindrop look more like a raindrop or how we could make storm clouds move like storm clouds."[14]

Walt hired art teacher Don Graham to teach animation and drawing to his employees. Artists studied and drew animals moving. They sketched people and made caricatures.

Walt wanted his staff to know the mechanics of drawing. Most of all, he wanted to make films that made moviegoers laugh.

The Duck, Pluto, and the Goof

New characters kept joining the Disney cartoon family. Pluto (1930), a clumsy, amiable dog, made people laugh at his antics. He once got stuck, nose to tail, on flypaper.[15] Goofy (1932) was a good-natured, but dimwitted, human character with doglike characteristics. Donald Duck (1934) was conceited, with a terrible temper and an unintelligible quacking voice.

Walt joked that Mickey Mouse, the most popular character of all, did not mind helping the newcomers. "The Mouse knows we have to keep bringing new people along, new faces," Walt explained. "It makes his job that much easier. It was pretty tough when he was carrying the whole studio. But now he's got The Duck and Pluto and The Goof and our feature program. Quite an accomplishment for a mouse."[16]

moccasins, and comfortable slacks. Walt smoked cigarettes heavily (in those days, the dangers of smoking were not known), and people could hear his trademark deep cough as he approached. When he talked, he wrapped a lock of his thick dark hair around his finger—when he was not jumping around explaining an idea. If Walt started to drum his long fingers, animators knew they had to rethink their ideas and start over.

Walt tried not to bother his animators while they were working. But late at night, he would peek at work left on their desks. Sometimes he pulled discarded drawings from the wastebasket. If he liked what he found, he left notes, telling artists not to throw away their good ideas.[17]

One night in early 1934, Walt called several animators together. For the next two hours, Walt acted out all the parts in the Grimm's fairy tale "Snow

White and the Seven Dwarfs." He was the Evil Queen, mixing poison for the apple she planned to give to Snow White. One by one, he became each of the Seven Dwarfs as they decided what to do about "the awful Thing in their house [Snow White]," as Walt wrote in a summary of the story.[18] By the time Walt's Snow White awoke, having been kissed by the handsome Prince, Walt had convinced his creative staff that the studio should make its first feature-length cartoon. The story had all the right elements—romance, drama, humor, and sympathetic characters.[19]

Roy Disney was nervous about the estimated $500,000 the movie would cost. Walt's attitude was, "A buck is something to be spent creating."[20] The two brothers had always disagreed about finances. Yet Walt was fiercely loyal to his brother and knew that Roy's caution was valuable to the studio's success.

When Hollywood experts heard about Walt's plans, they did not think audiences would sit through a ninety-minute cartoon film. Some critics called *Snow White and the Seven Dwarfs* "Disney's Folly."[21]

The physical appearances and personalities of the characters emerged. Talented artist Joe Grant designed the Evil Queen and the Wicked Witch. The team debated about the Seven Dwarfs' names. Rejected names included Shifty, Nifty, Woeful, Soulful, Flabby, Crabby, Awful, and Snoopy. Finally, the group agreed on six names: Doc, Grumpy, Happy, Sleepy, Sneezy, and Bashful. For a long time, the seventh and youngest Dwarf was "Seven." Finally, he became Dopey.[22]

In 1935, to celebrate their tenth anniversaries, Roy and Walt took their wives to Europe. On their vacation, the couples checked on European audiences' responses to Disney films. Some movie theaters showed several Mickey Mouse cartoons in a row. Audiences seemed to have no trouble paying attention.

Walt was excited about using color in his cartoons.

From 1934 to 1937, Disney Studio produced sixty-four cartoons and won five Academy Awards. The first Mickey Mouse cartoon in color also came out. In late 1936 and early 1937, Walt produced the Silly Symphony called *The Old Mill.* For this film, animators used a new invention, the multiplane camera. It helped viewers see depth on the flat screen, making some figures seem closer than others.

Walt and Lilly wanted more children, but after Diane's birth, Lilly had another miscarriage. So in January 1937, the Disneys adopted Sharon Mae Disney. Like other wealthy families, the Disneys hired a nurse to help Lillian care for the children. Protective of their children, they did not let newspapers publish information or photos about them. When Lilly and Walt were out or away, only their trusted relatives or friends watched the children.

Over the three years it took to complete *Snow White and the Seven Dwarfs,* artists made two million drawings to create eighty-three minutes of film. Six hundred people worked on the movie. It took six months to create the scene where the Seven Dwarfs march though the woods singing, "Heigh-ho, heigh-ho, it's off to work we go . . . " Meanwhile the cost of the film ballooned from the initial estimate of $500,000 to $1.5 million. Roy pleaded with the bank to give the studio more credit. Although Walt still wanted to fix every glitch, he could not. The film had to be out in time for Christmas.

On December 21, 1937, *Snow White and the Seven Dwarfs* made its debut at the Carthay Theater in Los Angeles. Famous actors attended. In the last scene, Snow White appears to be dead, poisoned by the Evil Queen's apple. Birds drop rose petals. Dwarfs draw close and dab their eyes. The audience cried, too. The grief-stricken Prince gently kisses Snow White as she lies in the coffin. When her eyes fluttered open, the audience stood and cheered. For the first time, a full-length cartoon had touched people's hearts.

For the movie *Snow White and the Seven Dwarfs*, artists made 2 million drawings. In this picture, Doc and Bashful are having a conversation.

For four weeks, *Snow White and the Seven Dwarfs* ran at Radio City Music Hall in New York City. Soon it opened at movie theaters all over the country. Reviewer Frank Nugent rated the film as one of the "ten best pictures of 1938."[23] Children knew all Seven Dwarfs by name. Songs like "Some Day My Prince Will Come" and "Whistle While You Work" played on radio stations across the nation. Within six months, the movie had earned $8 million. With movie ticket prices averaging 25 cents for adults and 10 cents for children, this meant huge numbers of viewers. With the profits, Roy paid off the studio's loans.

Walt maintained that children love to be scared. His daughter Diane has a vivid memory from childhood of being almost five and watching *Snow White and the Seven Dwarfs* on a Disney sound stage. "When the queen drank the potion and turned into a witch, I began to scream. . . . the next thing I knew I was outside in the sun. . . ." Diane's father later said of the incident, "Yes, she was scared, but I saw her peeking through her fingers." Later, Walt's daughters' favorite game became "Old Witch," which they played with their uncle Bill Cottrell, a Disney employee who was married to Lillian's sister Hazel.[24]

One day Diane came home from school and asked her father if he was *the* Walt Disney her friends talked about. When he said yes, she asked for his autograph.

"We loved our daddy so much," said Diane.[25]

All the Disneys except Ruth now lived in Los Angeles. At their sons' urging, Flora and Elias had relocated from Portland to Los Angeles. On weekends, the families would get together to play croquet and eat hamburgers and corn on the cob.

In 1937, Flora and Elias Disney celebrated their fiftieth wedding anniversary with four of their children and five grandchildren. With a studio tape recorder, Walt interviewed Flora and Elias about their life and marriage.

In the fall of 1938, Walt and Roy moved their aging parents into a small house they had bought for them and hired a housekeeper to make their lives more comfortable. On the night of November 26, 1938, gas from a faulty furnace seeped throughout Elias and Flora's home. The housekeeper found Elias and Flora upstairs, unconscious from the gas fumes. A neighbor helped drag the couple outside. Elias survived; Flora did not.

Devastated, the family mourned for Flora, the warm heart of the Disney family. At work, Walt and Roy said very little to anyone about their family's tragedy. Even years later, he still had a hard time talking about it.[26] Walt buried his sorrow in working on new projects.

9
FANTASY
& WAR

By the end of 1938, Walt and his studio were working on three new feature films. In the well-known story *Pinocchio*, written by Carlo Collodi in 1881, a wooden puppet longs to be a real live boy. Disney artists made working models of clocks and toys so they could study their movements. They practiced sketching ocean scenes. "We cannot do the fantastic . . . unless we first know the real," said Walt.[1]

Pinocchio became one of the most complex animated films yet, filled with rich details and amazing designs. In the early stages, Walt complained that the puppet's personality was dull and that Pinocchio acted like a spoiled child. Walt thought the story needed extra characters to add interest—the kindly Geppetto, the wily Honest John, the wise Blue Fairy, and the evil puppeteer,

Stromboli. Disney animators and artists decided their cricket, named Jiminy, would act as Pinocchio's conscience. When Pinocchio was unkind to Geppetto, the wood-carver who had created him, Jiminy Cricket scolded Pinocchio. Whenever Pinocchio lied, his nose grew longer.

Animator Ward Kimball turned Jiminy into a cricket that looked more like a man than a bug. Jiminy Cricket had a sassy attitude, wore a top hat, suit, and gloves, and carried a large umbrella.

Fantasia combined classical music with animation and took the studio in a new direction. Walt asked famed conductor Leopold Stokowski to adapt familiar classical pieces by well-known composers to fit *Fantasia's* story line. Ludwig van Beethoven's *Symphony No. 6*, called the *Pastoral* symphony, became a story about the Greek gods. Igor Stravinsky's *Rite of Spring* told about the birth of the earth and the dinosaur age. Happy hippos wearing lacy

Disney kept close tabs on his animators. This artist is working on an action scene for Jiminy Cricket in *Pinocchio*.

pink tutus danced a ballet to the music of Amilcare Ponchielli's *Dance of the Hours.*

"Music is dramatic," Walt said. "It is often more expressive than words can be."[2]

Mickey Mouse starred in *Fantasia* as an assistant to a sorcerer, a wizard. Mickey does not always use the sorcerer's magic wisely. Mickey gets into mischief, with a broomstick and bucket as accomplices.

The third movie in production at this time was *Bambi*, filled with humor, warmth, danger, and sadness. Set in a forest, the story features a mother deer and her young fawn, Bambi. The father deer is nearby, but trying to hide from hunters. The mother deer strips bark from trees to feed her fawn. A playful rabbit, Thumper, teaches Bambi a lesson how to skate on a frozen pond. The movie also stars a lovable skunk, Flower, and a wise friend, Owl.

> **"Music is dramatic. It is often more expressive than words can be."**

Many of the artists creating *Bambi* had never drawn realistic-looking animals. Walt had live deer brought onto the studio lot, where they munched on hay in the middle of a big room. With drawing pads in hand, the artists studied the animals' motions and drew what they observed.

Walt's daughter Diane cried when she saw a cut of the film and realized the mother deer dies. She wanted to know why her daddy could not leave out that part. Walt had no good answer for his daughter. He did not hesitate to make a point even if it made children sad. The mother deer's death stayed in the movie.

In 1939, the Disney brothers built a brand-new, $3 million headquarters in Burbank, California, near Hollywood. The spacious building had volleyball and badminton courts, a gym on the roof, plant-filled grounds with park benches, and a restaurant that even delivered lunches to employees.

Artists had always called the rooms where they worked and screened their films "sweatboxes." Now finally, they could work in air-conditioned comfort. But the term "sweatboxes" stuck. They still sweated, worrying whether Walt would like their work. Critical and difficult to please, he often lost his temper: "I used to get mad and blow my top—kind of a Donald-Duck-type-thing," Walt admitted.[3] His temper made people afraid to bring up new ideas during brainstorming sessions. If Walt did not like an idea, he yelled in front of everybody. The staff also knew that Walt did not like dirty jokes or gossip.

To avoid his outbursts, employees borrowed a line from *Bambi* as a secret code: "Man is in the forest." If Walt was close by, somebody might sound a warning, yelling, "Man's in the forest!"[4]

Walt also had a kind, soft side. He gave time and money to charities. He remembered the names of his

© Disney Enterprises, Inc.

Every year, new characters were added to the Disney cartoons.

employees' wives and children. If someone had a baby, he sent flowers. When animator Ollie Johnston fell ill, Walt paid Johnston's salary and told him to take as much time as he needed to recover.

Walt's brain was constantly dreaming up new ideas, and he wanted everybody at Disney to continue learning and growing as well. He arranged for architect Frank Lloyd Wright and other consultants to give lectures and classes at the studio.

In September 1939, Germany's dictator Adolf Hitler sent soldiers to invade Poland. This marked the beginning of World War II in Europe. Walt Disney's overseas movie markets dried up, cutting the studio's profits in half. With fifteen hundred employees and a whopping $4.5-million debt, the studio entered a financial crisis. Workers wondered who might be given layoff notices.

Both *Pinocchio* and *Fantasia* premiered in 1940. But neither movie made as much money as *Snow White and the Seven Dwarfs*, which did not help the company's financial problems. *Pinocchio* did win two Oscars for that year, one for the best musical score, and one for the classic song "When You Wish Upon a Star."

Audiences' reactions to *Fantasia* were lukewarm. Moviegoers were not used to hearing classical music in a cartoon. The film's distributor suggested cutting the movie from two hours to eighty-two minutes. Walt refused.

One day in 1940, Walt had a surprise visitor—Ub Iwerks. Ten years before, Ub had left Walt Disney Studio to form his own cartoon company. It had done well—until lately. After they talked, Walt again hired Ub. He was a technical genius as well as a highly skilled animator. Ub helped the studio improve its lenses and coloring methods to make cartoons more lifelike. Walt recognized and appreciated Ub's huge contributions to the company—inventions, innovations, and patents, some still in use today.[5]

Walt had always thought of the Disney staff as one big family. But across the country, many workers were joining labor unions. Members of the Screen Cartoonists Guild hoped that Disney's artists and animators would join, too. Though Walt paid his people well, his artistic staff wanted other benefits that unions could offer.

Walt chose to let the company lawyer, a man not known for his tact, negotiate between Disney workers and Walt. In February 1941, Walt finally spoke to his employees directly in a long meeting. He explained the studio's financial difficulties and urged his employees not to unionize.

Despite Walt's efforts, on May 28, 1941, most of Disney's workers went on strike. Walt thought the strike would last just days. Instead it lasted weeks. Picketers held signs and shouted outside the studio. Some accused Walt of living a lavish lifestyle on Disney profits. The truth was that most of Walt's money was tied up in his corporation.

In the fall of 1941, the U.S. government asked Walt to go to South America on a goodwill tour. He agreed, but only if he could do some film work there. Lilly, her sister Hazel, and eighteen artists, animators, and musicians went along. Two films, *The Three Caballeros* and *Saludos Amigos,* resulted from the film footage made there. Everywhere he went, Walt entertained people, even standing on his head once to make people laugh.[6] During the trip, Walt received sad news—his father had died. After Flora Disney's death three years before, Elias Disney had lost his will to live.

By the time Walt returned from South America, the strike had ended. Walt's attitude toward employees changed. From then on, they had to punch a time clock. Fringe benefits, like catered lunches, disappeared. Several artists left the studio. Walt said about the strike, "It was the toughest period I've had in my whole life."[7]

Despite the chaos, the studio completed a sixty-four-minute cartoon film called *Dumbo.* The movie had a strong plot. A feisty stork delivers Dumbo to his proud mother, a circus elephant. Her baby, designed by artist Bill Peet, is bright-eyed and appealing with gigantic, floppy ears. Dumbo soon discovers that his ears make perfect wings for flying.[8]

World War II: Everyone's War

After Japan's attack on Pearl Harbor on December 7, 1941, America entered World War II. Comic strip characters, like Superman and Popeye the Sailor Man, urged Americans to get behind the war effort. Many Hollywood studios began making war movies. By 1945, when World War II ended, 405,399 U.S. soldiers had died, plus thousands of soldiers and civilians in other countries. Eleven million people died in the concentration camps of Germany's dictator, Adolf Hitler.

The U.S. government enlisted Mickey Mouse and the Disney Studio to join the war effort during World War II.

APPRECIATE ★ AMERICA

"COME ON GANG – ALL OUT FOR UNCLE SAM" Mickey

©WDP

BUY UNITED STATES DEFENSE BONDS AND SAVINGS STAMPS

© Disney Enterprises, Inc.

The movie opened on Halloween in 1941, and soon its memorable songs were being played on the radio. *Dumbo* was scheduled to be the cover story for *Time* magazine in early December. But on December 7, 1941, the Japanese attacked the U.S. Naval base at Pearl Harbor, Oahu, Hawaii. The next day, President Franklin Roosevelt declared war on Japan. News of the Pearl Harbor attack filled newspapers and magazines. Disney's magazine cover featuring *Dumbo* never appeared.

The government suspected the West Coast might be attacked next. After the Pearl Harbor attack, a U.S. military division set up its headquarters at Walt Disney Studio. To make room for seven hundred soldiers, the staff doubled up and shared offices. The military had chosen Disney's studio because it was close to a key weapons plant. Disney was asked to create cartoons, live photography, and many other types of films for the war effort. "We did anything they wanted," Walt said.[9]

Disney made military cartoons starring familiar characters like Donald Duck, Goofy, Jiminy Cricket, and the Seven Dwarfs. In *Der Fuehrer's Face*, Donald Duck dreamed about working in a German factory. He got mad at Adolf Hitler and threw tomatoes at a photo of the dictator. Troops used "Mickey Mouse" as a code word during a key invasion.[10] On the cover of a July 1942 Walt Disney comic book, Goofy and Donald Duck carried an American flag.

With soldiers camped out in the studio's halls and offices, Walt's patience wore thin.[11] Still, the studio created films like *Victory Through Air Power*, described by one newspaper as "an excellent propaganda film" and "a sixty-five-minute lecture."[12]

Work on all nonmilitary projects had stopped, except for the movie *Bambi*, which reached theaters on August 21, 1942. Rave reviews followed, and *Bambi* made money immediately. Finally, there was happy news in the midst of grim war realities.

Not everyone loved *Bambi*; for instance, deer hunters resented it. Walt said of the hunters: "They didn't dare come home and brag to their family that they'd shot a deer."[13]

10

"ZIP-A-DEE-DOO-DAH!"

In 1945, World War II ended, leaving Walt eager to plunge into new ventures, though costs rose for each new film. Roy advised caution; the war had left the company deeply in debt.

Sometimes the brothers' arguments about the Disney Studio's future exploded into shouting matches. During one argument, Roy said, "Walt, you're letting this place drive you nuts. That's one place I'm not going with you."[1] Roy stomped out. Neither Walt nor Roy slept much that night. The next morning, they patched up their differences with a few gruff words.

Had it not been for the strong bond between Roy and Walt, their working partnership would never have survived. Walt's nephew, Roy Edward Disney, said later of

© Disney Enterprises, Inc.

Disney met with songwriter Johnny Mercer to work on *Song of the South*, based on the Uncle Remus tales.

them, "If they hadn't been brothers, this thing [the studio] would have fallen apart in the first ten minutes."[2]

Between 1946 and 1948, the studio worked on a series of animated short pieces set to music. Flawed by sketchy plots, these films lacked the quality of earlier films. Critics sniped that perhaps Disney had lost its touch.

Walt Disney forged ahead, jumping into live-action films with *Song of the South*, based on the Uncle Remus tales he had read and loved as a child. Walt asked veteran Disney staff artist and storyteller Bill Peet to turn the original characters of Brer Rabbit, Brer Fox, and Brer Bear into cartoon figures. Peet described the work as "the most fun I'd had since *Dumbo*."

During story sessions for *Song of the South*, Peet described his boss: "I had seen the grumpy, bearish Walt and the jovial, good-natured one. . . . on the Remus fables, Walt was always in a good humor, full of enthusiasm . . . and the animators caught the playful spirit in preparing the fables for the screen."[3]

Most of the actors Walt hired for the film were African-American, including Oscar-winning actress Hattie McDaniel as Aunt Tempy. As Uncle Remus, actor James Baskett told the fables to a small boy. Around them, Brer Fox and other animated characters came to life.

> **Walt Disney forged ahead, jumping into live-action films.**

When *Song of the South* was released in 1946, some called it a warm family tale. Others, including the National Urban League, criticized it for casting African Americans as servants."[4]

Despite the controversy it caused, Walt was pleased with *Song of the South*.[5] One of its songs, the peppy, upbeat "Zip-a-Dee-Doo-Dah," won an Oscar in 1947.

The studio embarked on another new venture when Walt hired a photography team to film wildlife in

Walt Disney takes a picture of his daughters, Sharon, left, and Diane, in the family garden.

Alaska. Their many reels of film became a documentary about seals, *Seal Island*, the first in Disney's True-Life Adventures series. The film had music, clever writing, good editing, and humor. When the female seals arrive, the song "Here Comes the Bride" plays. As a male seal suns himself on a rock, a voice says, "What more could one wish? A good home, adoring wives. A peaceful paradise."[6] In the 1948 Academy Awards, *Seal Island* won in the Short Subject category.

Over the years, Walt had developed the hobby of creating intricate wood miniatures—stagecoaches, furniture, and trains. A studio carpenter had taught Walt how to use woodworking tools. Whenever possible, he would slip off to his workshop, crank up his circular saw, and work.

Fun Time with Daddy

"Daddy was our playmate. When he came home at night, that was fun time," said his daughter Diane.[7] On Sundays, Walt took Diane and Sharon to the zoo, the circus, or the park for unhurried afternoons spent playing and riding on the carousel. He taught Sharon and Diane to ride horseback and swim. Whatever his daughters did, he made them feel wonderful and talented. If they misbehaved, Sharon said, "He didn't spank. All he had to do was raise that eyebrow and we knew . . ."[8]

Walt and Lilly rarely fought. But once, at a Fourth of July picnic, a friend offered Walt a baby goat. Walt thought it would make a great pet; his daughters agreed. Walt loaded it into the family's small car with Lilly, her sister Grace, and his daughters. Once on the road, Lilly burst into tears; she wanted nothing to do with a hairy, smelly goat. Walt grew angry. Finally, to their daughters' disappointment, Walt agreed not to keep the goat.[9]

"Walt always liked to do things with his hands," said Disney animator Frank Thomas.[10]

"He was like a little boy," said animator Ward Kimball.[11]

In 1949 Walt and Lilly built a new house in Beverly Hills that reflected forty-eight-year-old Walt's playfulness. It included a movie theater, a playroom, and a soda fountain. There, according to Kimball, Walt whipped up "these big tall things with whipped cream and cherries. They'd be a mile high."[12]

The house's most unusual feature was a shiny, steam-driven black train with red and gold trim. Trains had always been fascinating to Walt.[13] Though one-eighth the size of a real train, Walt's train was big enough for people to ride in. Its half-mile track wound through fruit trees and through a 120-foot-long tunnel.

In the summer of 1949, Walt and Lilly took a two-month trip to Europe with Diane, fifteen, and Sharon, twelve. In Paris, Walt surprised the girls with boxes of mechanical toys—little dogs that did tricks, monkeys that beat on drums, and others. He wound them all up, sending toys clattering and banging all over the hotel room floor. Walt was the most intrigued, as he studied the mechanisms that made the toys move.

In England, the Disneys stayed near the set of Disney's first all live-action film, *Treasure Island*. Walt watched artists paint backgrounds that suggested any setting—a harbor, a castle, a pirate ship. He spent five weeks interacting with the actors and watching the cameramen work.

"As soon as Walt rode on a camera crane, we knew we were going to lose him," said one artist.[14] To Walt, live-action moviemaking seemed simpler than creating an animated cartoon.

Like others of his era, Walt's formal education had ended with the ninth grade. At forty-eight, he still struggled with grammar and pronunciation, and his secretary had to correct his spelling. Yet Walt hungered for knowledge and absorbed new information quickly. On a visit to Radio City Music Hall in New York City, he went backstage and studied the ropes, pulleys, and moving parts that made the sets for different scenes work.

He and Lilly often went out to the airport to watch planes land and take off. When on a plane, he enjoyed visiting the cockpit. According to Lillian Disney, "[Walt's] mind was never inactive."[15] Walt's niece Marjorie described her uncle as "a sponge, a human sponge."[16]

11

THE MAGIC KINGDOM

"**My brother was a kid all his life,**" Walt's sister Ruth once said.[1] Walt threw himself into each new creative project with child-like enthusiasm.

Walt had long been dreaming about creating a large park where families could go for entertainment. In Copenhagen, Denmark, he had visited Tivoli Gardens. The squeals of happy children filled this magical park. It had twinkling lights, flowers, rides, puppet shows, concerts, booths, and good restaurants. Tivoli Gardens was also reasonably priced and clean. He hoped to build such a place—called Disneyland Park—in America.

People told Walt that he would lose money on it, especially if he did not serve liquor or have a Ferris wheel. Roy Disney thought Walt should not try to compete in a business he knew nothing about.

Walt believed in his idea, so he formed a separate company, WED Enterprises (named after himself, Walter Elias Disney) as a research and development organization. Walt and his two daughters were the only stockholders. From other parts of his studio, he assembled a team of designers, architects, engineers, writers, and artists to begin planning the park. He also hired three model makers, headed by Fred Joerger. They and others became known as Imagineers, combining imagination and engineering to develop the rides. They turned two-dimensional designs into three-dimensional models. The first models Joerger made for

Disney was eager to share his ideas for Disneyland Park.

Television: Something New in People's Homes

Television came about because of the inventions of many different people working independently in the United States and the rest of the world. Americans Alexander Graham Bell, Thomas Edison, and Philo Farnsworth all contributed to the electronic version of television that first appeared in the 1920s and 1930s. By 1950, there were 4.4 million televisions in the United States, and that number kept increasing. Some filmmakers and critics feared that as television's popularity grew, people would stay home and watch television rather than go to movie theaters.

Walt Disney welcomed television. Instead of having to convince theater owners to show his films, he could take them straight to the viewing public.

Disneyland Park were for Main Street, U.S.A., the steamboat *Mark Twain*, and the Jungle Cruise.[2]

After careful research, Walt purchased 180 acres of orange and avocado groves in Anaheim, California, close to Los Angeles. Turning the land into a magic kingdom in just two years seemed impossible. "It's kind of fun to do the impossible," Walt explained.[3]

As the park progressed, Walt was at the site most days, making suggestions. "He [Walt] wanted to see every idea that you could possibly have before he settled on something," said one designer.[4]

Walt decided to use television to build financial support and ensure the Disneyland Park's success. In December 1950, Walt's first show, *One Hour in Wonderland*, aired. It included clips from his upcoming *Alice in Wonderland* movie. The viewers liked it; another show followed the next year.

Walt began planning a weekly one-hour show. Roy

found a New York network, ABC, to sponsor it. ABC agreed to pay Walt Disney Studio $500,000 and promised loans of up to $4.5 million, in exchange for a one-third interest in Disneyland Park.

Walt's first weekly television show ran on October 27, 1954. Succeeding episodes were a mixture of fantasy, adventure, education, and drama, and sometimes, already released film and cartoons. Through hints and announcements, Walt built people's interest in the park. He filmed in color, even though most American television sets were black and white. Walt already imagined a time when all televisions would be in color. When that happened, Disney would be ready.

Walt continued to oversee the many movies the studio was making.

Producer Jerry Wald once said of Walt, "Disney has eyes that see what no other man sees. He can look at a bird's awkward mating dance and

Cinderella

For *Cinderella*, released in 1950, Walt and his talented staff took the familiar story of the cinder maid who became a princess and turned it into an animated film.

Ilene Woods, Cinderella's singing voice, remembered Walt brainstorming with her about a song called "Sing Sweet Nightingale," which Cinderella sings while scrubbing the floor. Walt suggested having Cinderella appear in three different "bubbles," as she sang in three-part harmony. Engineers recorded Ilene's voice singing one part. Then wearing earphones, she harmonized with her own voice two more times to create the harmony.

"To me, he [Walt] was a true visionary, " Ilene said. "Others would say 'Can we?' and Walt would say, 'We can.' "[5]

choreograph it into a comic ballet in one of his nature films; he can stare at a doorknob and, by adding a mouth here and ears there, can convert it into one of the most engaging characters. . . ."[7]

When he was not thinking about movies and television shows, Walt's mind was on Disneyland Park. Harrison Ellenshaw, the son of the great Disney artist Peter Ellenshaw, remembered riding a handcart with Walt on the park's unfinished railroad. "From a ten-year-old's point of view, it was amazing to see this grown man getting as big a thrill out of riding that flatbed as I was. I remember seeing this big grin on his face."[8]

Some ideas did not work or had to be changed. For the *Mark Twain* riverboat ride, workers had dug out and created a river. It kept running dry until the bottom was relined with clay. Walt had wanted to use real animals for the Jungle Cruise, but soon realized that they might be asleep or uncooperative when visitors came. The real animals were replaced with mechanized ones. Even so, there were problems. Sometimes the mechanical giraffe got stuck

Diane Disney Marries Ron Miller

Early in 1954, Walt and Lilly's daughter Diane married Ron Miller, a professional football player. "Daddy led me down the aisle and stood with me," Diane said later. "I heard this sob, turned around, and Daddy was standing there with tears streaming down his cheeks."[6]

For the wedding cake, Walt designed a bride and a groom wearing tennis shoes, Bermuda shorts, and sweatshirts. Diane's husband, Ron, eventually worked for Walt as an associate producer.

chewing leaves. One of the biggest challenges was hoisting a nine-hundred-pound mechanical elephant into place.

On July 13, 1955, Walt and Lilly celebrated thirty years of marriage at the almost-finished park. For a few hours, they relaxed, enjoyed dinner with family and friends, danced, and looked around.

Opening day was just days away. Yet workers were still connecting pipes in restrooms. Painters were still putting finishing coats on bare walls. On July 17, 1955, the park's opening was televised live, with viewers all over the country watching. Despite numerous problems and throngs of people overflowing the park, Walt's dream park opened with fanfare, speeches, a dedication, music, and splashy ceremonies. In its first seven and a half weeks, Disneyland Park had a whopping one million visitors.

Walt Disney had succeeded in creating a magical kingdom for children and adults. With it, he drew

Opening day was just days away. Yet workers were still connecting pipes in restrooms.

children and adults into fairy tales and nostalgia they could see and touch, with each experience a new story.

Time magazine featured Walt Disney in its December 27, 1954, issue.

12

END OF AN ERA

After Disneyland Park's splashy opening, Walt kept tinkering—finding ways to make the park more beautiful. He and Lilly often stayed overnight in their apartment above the Fire House on Disneyland Park's Main Street. Walt, fifty-four, roamed through the park, checking rides, restrooms, even burned-out light bulbs, and watching to see that his employees treated visitors politely. Many people recognized him, so he sometimes wore sunglasses and a broad-brimmed hat as a disguise.

The fresh-faced young performers who had welcomed visitors on opening day became known as the Mouseketeers. Walt wanted them to look like ordinary neighborhood kids. They wore uniforms that included white T-shirts printed with their names and beanie caps with Mickey Mouse ears. A daily ABC television show, *The Mickey Mouse Club*, debuted on October 3, 1955. The group's trademark sign-off song began by spelling out the name of everybody's favorite mouse, "M-I-C (see you real soon) K-E-Y (Why? Because we like you!") M-O-U-S-E!" Soon children all over America began tuning in.

On the set where the show was filmed, Walt told the Mouseketeers to call him "Uncle Walt." But some were so in awe of him that they called him "Mr. Disney."[1]

Another Disney television show in production at this time was *Zorro*, the tale of a Robin Hood–like figure who galloped about the West on horseback. Masked and dressed in black, Zorro left his calling card wherever he went—the letter "Z" slashed with his sword.

Meanwhile, Walt and Lilly were enjoying being grandparents. Their first grandson had been born in 1954. Soon the Disneys had seven grandchildren between their two daughters' families. (Sharon had married Bob Brown in 1959.) Diane's younger son became Walt's namesake—Walter Elias Disney Miller.

In the late 1950s, and early 1960s, Walt Disney Studio produced more hit movies. Disney chose good stories from books or historical tales for the movies the studio made.

Other films showed his simple, somewhat corny

sense of humor. In *The Absent-Minded Professor* (1961), the professor discovers an amazing material (called "flubber") that makes cars fly.

"All right. I'm corny,"[2] Walt admitted.

When asked about the secret to his success, he said, "I'm an optimist. I'm not in the business to make unhappy pictures. I love comedy too much. . . . I can still be amazed at the wonders of the world."[3] Because he respected and loved children, he avoided talking down to them.

For many years, Walt had tried to convince author

The Disneys enjoyed relaxing in the yard: from left, son-in-law Ron Miller, Sharon, Diane, Lillian, and Walt, with Diane and Ron's children.

P. L. Travers to let him make a movie based on her book *Mary Poppins.* Finally in 1960, Travers agreed. Walt, fifty-eight, cast Julie Andrews, a young Broadway actress with a pure, clear voice, as Mary Poppins, the nanny who floats down out of the sky carrying a talking umbrella. The film had dancing, animated cartoon characters, and wonderful songs, such as the fast-paced "Supercalifragilisticexpialidocious." Released in 1964, *Mary Poppins* became an instant, blockbuster hit, with thirteen Academy Award nominations. Julie Andrews won best actress.

Dick Van Dyke, cast in the movie as Bert, a loveable and energetic chimney sweep, said of Walt, "To work with him was one of the most serendipitous [lucky] things that ever happened to me. . . . he had the enthusiasm of a ten-year-old about the work."[4]

Walt was now in his mid-sixties, but his creative energy was in full force. For the 1964 World's Fair in New York City, he staged four exhibits—"it's a small world," Great Moments with Mr. Lincoln, the Carousel of Progress, and the Magic Skyway. Fifty million people saw them.

Increasingly, Walt found he could not be involved in every movie, every project. Still, his curiosity kept leading him in new directions, chasing new dreams.

In late 1965, he purchased 27,443 acres of land near Orlando, Florida, for $5 million. Here he planned to build an idealistic place, EPCOT (Experimental

Prototype Community Of Tomorrow), where people could work, play, and live. This project would be 150 times larger than Disneyland Park. It is now called Walt Disney World Resort.

By the mid-1960s, Walt had begun to have frequent backaches, colds, and sinus attacks. He had grown short of breath, and his skin color was often gray. In early November 1966, doctors took x-rays. The diagnosis was lung cancer, caused by years of smoking cigarettes.

After the removal of his left lung, doctors told Lilly and his daughters that Walt had only months to live. Ever the optimist, Walt believed there had to be some solution to this pesky problem. "He thought doctors were magicians," said Diane.[5]

Walt visited the studio, where he checked on movies in progress. He spent time with his family, and enjoyed his grandchildren at

Now & Then

In 1959, Disneyland Park expanded, and three new rides were added. At first, Walt had not wanted roller coasters in his park. But once the fourteen-story Matterhorn Mountain ride was built, Walt enjoyed inviting special visitors—comedians, kings, even presidents. At the ride's end, Walt chuckled when water splattered and surprised his guests.

The original 180 acres of orange groves that became Disneyland Park in 1955 have grown to more than 430 acres. Since opening day, more than 500,000,000 people have visited Disneyland Park. In its first fifty years, 78,617,280 pairs of Mickey Mouse Ears were sold.

The modern park has safaris, a rain forest, a roller coaster, and Broadway-quality shows. Today, Disney theme parks exist all over the world, including Japan, France, and China.

Disney characters © Disney Enterprises, Inc.

In 2001 Walt Disney World Resort in Florida celebrated the hundredth anniversary of Disney's birth.

Thanksgiving. Walt went back into the hospital on November 30.

Over the next few weeks, he grew weaker. He allowed only family members to visit. Roy spent long hours at Walt's bedside; they talked about business. When Walt was alone, his imagination spewed out plans for EPCOT center and the studio's future. But on December 15, 1966, Walt Disney, age sixty-five, died.

Nobody had expected Walt's death to come so soon, least of all Walt.[6] Family, friends, and staff were devastated. A newspaper cartoon showed Mickey Mouse, head in his hands, with tears in his eyes.[7] Disneyland Park lowered its flags to half-mast to honor its founder.

Author and friend Ray Bradbury said, "Walt was a bursting fountain, always running at full speed. . . . Walt left the world a thousand times better than when he arrived."[8]

Walt's friend and longtime staffer Joe Grant said, "It is the end of an era."[9]

Around the world, people remembered Walt for creating lovable, unsophisticated characters and unforgettable songs. His thirty-two Oscars were proof that "innovation was Disney's specialty."[10] He was the driving force behind what became an international family entertainment and media corporation, currently

EPCOT Center & Walt Disney World Resort

Walt Disney dreamed that EPCOT's residents would live in an experimental community surrounded by swaths of green grass. People could leave their cars at home because of a network of people-movers and monorails. One designer, Bob Gurr, was amazed at Walt's ability to think both big and small: "He [Walt] can see the big picture, but in his mind he still has the idea of a little detail . . . . And it's all done with a wave of a pencil and drawings."[11] Walt died before his EPCOT dream came to life. His dedicated brother Roy carried the project on. Groundbreaking for the EPCOT Center took place in 1967, and a modified version opened October 1, 1971. Roy Disney died a few months later.

While Walt's experimental city never came to pass, part of his dream became reality. Today the sprawling theme park, renamed Epcot, contains numerous international pavilions and offers imaginative adventures and fun for young and old.

involved in movies, theme parks and resorts, television, books, products, music, and animated films. Even today, "The only name you can drop without an explanation is Walt Disney . . ."[12]

Animator Ollie Johnson said of Walt, "The guy was all about entertainment."[13]

Walt Disney kept his promise to his father—he made the family name famous and changed the entertainment industry for the better.

With his legacy of beloved characters, theme parks, and films, Walt Disney continues to delight and entertain children and adults of all ages.

CHRONOLOGY

Walter Elias Disney born on December 5 in Chicago, Illinois.	**1901**
The Disneys move to a farm in Marceline, Missouri.	**1906**
Walt starts elementary school at Park School in Marceline.	**1909**
The Disneys move to Kansas City, Missouri. Walt attends Benton Grammar School, delivers newspapers, takes art lessons.	**1910– 1917**
Disney family moves to Chicago, Illinois; Walt enters McKinley High School.	**1917**
Works for the U.S. Post Office, takes art classes.	**1918**
Becomes a driver for the Red Cross Ambulance Corps.	**1918– 1919**
Moves to Kansas City, draws cartoons at a commercial art studio and a film ad company.	**1919– 1921**
Founds Laugh-O-grams, a cartoon business that eventually fails. Moves to Los Angeles, and sets up a studio in Uncle Robert Disney's garage. Walt and Roy go into business together.	**1922– 1923**
The first of 56 *Alice* cartoons is shown in movie theaters. Walt and Roy build a studio.	**1924**
Walt marries Lillian Bounds.	**1925**

1926   Disney Brothers move into their new studio.

1927   Disney's *Oswald the Lucky Rabbit*, their first all-cartoon film, is released.

1928   Mickey Mouse, with Walt providing Mickey's voice, appears in *Plane Crazy*, *The Gallopin' Gaucho*, and *Steamboat Willie*. Walt experiments with adding sound to cartoons. Mickey Mouse becomes an international star.

1929–
1930   *The Skeleton Dance*, the first of Disney's Silly Symphonies, is released. More Silly Symphonies follow. New cartoon character Pluto joins Mickey Mouse.

1932   Goofy makes his debut. The studio signs a contract with Technicolor. *Flowers and Trees* wins an Academy Award. *Three Little Pigs* is released.

1933   Diane Marie Disney is born on December 18.

1934   Studio expands to a staff of 200. Donald Duck makes his first appearance in *The Wise Little Hen*.

1934–
1937   The studio produces sixty-four cartoons, wins five Academy Awards, and releases the first Mickey Mouse cartoon in color. *Snow White*, Disney's first full-length feature cartoon, is released.

1937   Walt and Lillian adopt Sharon Mae Disney in January. *Snow White* debuts in December.

1938   Flora Disney dies on November 26. Walt and the studio work on *Fantasia*, *Pinocchio*, and *Bambi*.

1939   The Disneys build a $3-million headquarters in Burbank, California.

Disney workers go on strike. *Dumbo* is released. Elias Disney dies. **1940–1941**

The United States enters World War II. A military division moves into the studio. The studio makes war-related films. *Bambi* opens in theaters. **1942**

Make Mine Music is released. Walt moves into live-action and nature films, *Song of the South* and *Seal Island*, a True-Life Adventures film. **1946–1948**

Walt and his family travel to Europe. Walt visits the set of the Disney movie *Treasure Island* in England. **1949**

Cinderella, *Alice in Wonderland*, and *Peter Pan* are released. Walt moves into television. Disneyland Park opens in 1955. **1950–1955**

Sleeping Beauty and *The Shaggy Dog* are released. **1958–1959**

Mary Poppins, *The Incredible Journey*, *Swiss Family Robinson*, *The Sword in the Stone*, and several other films released. Establishes California Institute of the Arts and creates exhibits for the 1964 World's Fair. **1960–1964**

Purchases land in Florida for his EPCOT and theme park project. **1965**

Dies of lung cancer on December 15, leaving his wife, two daughters, seven grandchildren, and numerous nieces and nephews. **1966**

FILMS & TELEVISION SHOWS
CREATED DURING WALT DISNEY'S LIFETIME
A Selected List

1922—Laugh-O-grams (cartoon shorts)

1924–1927—56 *Alice* cartoons

1928—Mickey Mouse cartoons, including *Plane Crazy, The Gallopin' Gaucho, Steamboat Willie*

1929–1939—Silly Symphonies, 75 in all, including *The Skeleton Dance, Flowers and Trees, Three Little Pigs, The Old Mill*

1930–1937—Mickey and Friends appear in 120 cartoons, starring Mickey Mouse, joined later by Minnie Mouse, Donald Duck, Goofy, and Pluto.

1937—*Snow White and the Seven Dwarfs*

1938—*Ferdinand the Bull*

1940—*Pinocchio, Fantasia*

1941—*Dumbo*

1942—*Der Fuehrer's Face, Bambi*

1943—*Victory through Air Power*

1946—*Song of the South, Make Mine Music*

1948—*Seal Island*, the first of Disney's True-Life Adventures

1950—*Treasure Island, One Hour in Wonderland* (first television show), *Cinderella*

1951—*Alice in Wonderland*

1952—*The Story of Robin Hood*

1953—*The Living Desert*

1954—*20,000 Leagues Under the Sea, Rob Roy: The Highland Rogue, The Wonderful World of Disney* (Disney Television)

1955—*Davy Crockett: King of the Wild Frontier, Lady and the Tramp, The Mickey Mouse Club* (Disney Television)

1957—*Johnny Tremain, Zorro* (Disney Television)

1959—*Sleeping Beauty, The Shaggy Dog*

1960—*Pollyanna, Swiss Family Robinson*

1961—*The Absent-Minded Professor, The Parent Trap, Babes in Toyland, One Hundred and One Dalmatians*

1964—*Mary Poppins*

CHAPTER NOTES

Chapter 1. Walt's Big Idea

1. Katherine and Richard Greene, *The Man Behind the Magic: The Story of Walt Disney* (New York: Viking, 1998), p. 44.

2. Ibid., p. 128.

3. Arthur Levine, "Looking Back at Disneyland: Reminiscing During Disneyland's 50th Anniversary," (n.d.), <http://themeparks.about.com/od/disneyparks/a/DL50quotes.htm> (August 13, 2005).

4. Greene, *The Man Behind the Magic: The Story of Walt Disney*, p. 129.

5. "More Magical Memories," *San Diego Westways Southern California Lifestyle Magazine*, May/June 2005 (see back issues online, May/June 2005 issue), <http://www.aaa-calif. com/westways/0505/features/magicalmemories.asp> (February 24, 2006).

6. Kimi Yoshino, "A Landmark's Landmark," *Los Angeles Times: Calendar Weekend*, May 5, 2005, pp. E4–5.

7. Kimi Yoshino & Dave McKibben, "Disneyland Marks Its Big 5-0," *Los Angeles Times*, May 6, 2005, pp. B1, 10.

8. "More Magical Memories."

9. Author interview with Connie Plantz, August 26, 2005.

10. "Father Goose," *Time*, December 27, 1954, pp. 42–46.

Chapter 2. Childhood & Farm Life

1. Bob Thomas, *Walt Disney: An American Original* (New York: Disney Editions, 1994), p. 25.

2. Ibid., p. 27.

3. Diane Disney Miller with Pete Martin, "My Dad Walt Disney: Part II," *The Saturday Evening Post*, November 24, 1956, p. 70.

4. John Flinn, "Get the Inside Dish on Disneyland," *The Bakersfield Californian*, May 8, 2005, p. H2.

5. Thomas, p. 29.

6. Katherine and Richard Greene, *The Man Behind the Magic: The Story of Walt Disney* (New York: Viking, 1998), p. 8.

7. Ibid., p. 10.

8. Ibid.

9. Ibid., p. 15.

10. Miller, "My Dad Walt Disney: Part II," p. 70.

11. "Marceline Missouri: Boyhood Home of Walt Disney," (n.d.), <http://www.marceline.org> (December 15, 2005).

Chapter 3. Newspaper Boy & Emerging Actor

1. "Father Goose," *Time*, December 27, 1954, p. 44.

2. Diane Disney Miller with Pete Martin, "My Dad Walt Disney: Part II," *The Saturday Evening Post*, November 24, 1956, p. 70.

3. Katherine and Richard Greene, *The Man Behind the Magic: The Story of Walt Disney* (New York: Viking, 1998), p. 14.

4. Ibid., p. 13.

5. Bob Thomas, *Walt Disney: An American Original* (New York: Disney Editions, 1994, p. 34.

6. Ibid., p. 35.

7. Katherine and Richard Greene, *Inside the Dream: The Personal Story of Walt Disney* (New York: Roundtable Press, 2001), p. 27.

8. Katherine and Richard Greene, *The Man Behind the Magic: The Story of Walt Disney* (New York: Viking, 1998), p. 16.

9. Amy Boothe Green and Howard E. Green, *Remembering Walt: Favorite Memories of Walt Disney*, p. 6.

10. Thomas, pp. 38–39.

11. Miller, "My Dad Walt Disney: Part II," p. 70.

12. Thomas, pp. 38–39.

13. Thomas, p. 39.

Chapter 4. Chasing His Dream in Chicago

1. Katherine and Richard Greene, *The Man Behind the Magic: The Story of Walt Disney* (New York: Viking, 1998), p. 22.

2. Bob Thomas, *Walt Disney: An American Original* (New York: Disney Editions, 1994,) p. 42.

3. Ibid., p. 42.

4. Ibid., p. 45.

5. Greene, *The Man Behind the Magic: The Story of Walt Disney*, p. 23.

6. Thomas, p. 44.

7. Greene, *The Man Behind the Magic: The Story of Walt Disney*, p. 23.

8. Ibid., pp. 23–24.

9. Thomas, p. 46.

10. Greene, *The Man Behind the Magic: The Story of Walt Disney*, p. 26.

11. Ibid.

Chapter 5. Laugh-O-grams: A Good Hard Failure

1. Bob Thomas, *Walt Disney: An American Original* (New York: Disney Editions, 1994,) p. 55.

2. Ibid., p. 58.

3. Ibid., p. 61.

4. Katherine and Richard Greene, *The Man Behind the Magic: The Story of Walt Disney* (New York: Viking, 1998), p. 41.

5. Diane Disney Miller with Pete Martin, "My Dad Walt Disney: Part II," *The Saturday Evening Post*, November 24, 1956, p. 80.

6. Greene, *The Man Behind the Magic: The Story of Walt Disney*, p. 41.

7. Ibid., p. 37.

Chapter 6. Hello, Hollywood!

1. Diane Disney Miller with Pete Martin, "My Dad Walt Disney: Part III," *The Saturday Evening Post*, December 1, 1956, p. 29.

2. Katherine and Richard Greene, *The Man Behind the Magic: The Story of Walt Disney* (New York: Viking, 1998), p. 42.

3. Bob Thomas, *Walt Disney: An American Original* (New York: Disney Editions, 1994,) p. 74.

4. Greene, *The Man Behind the Magic: The Story of Walt Disney*, p. 46.

5. Miller, "My Dad Walt Disney: Part III," p. 71.

6. Ibid., p. 70.

7. Greene, *The Man Behind the Magic: The Story of Walt Disney*, p. 48.

8. Ibid., p. 49.

9. Thomas, pp. 78–80.

10. Katherine and Richard Greene, *Inside the Dream: The Personal Story of Walt Disney* (New York: Roundtable Press, 2001), p. 93.

11. "Father Goose," *Time*, December 27, 1954, p. 44.

12. Ibid., p. 44.

13. Greene, *The Man Behind the Magic: The Story of Walt Disney*, p. 53.

14. Miller, "My Dad Walt Disney: Part III," p. 75.

15. Douglas W. Churchill, "Now Mickey Mouse Enters Art's Temple," *The New York Times Magazine*, June 3, 1934, p. 12.

16. Miller, "My Dad Walt Disney: Part III," p. 75.

Chapter 7. Mickey Mouse Springs to Life!

1. "Father Goose," *Time*, December 27, 1954, p. 45.

2. "The Dream Merchant," *The New York Times*, December 16, 1966, p. 40.

3. <http://www.disney.go.com/disneyatoz/familymuseum/collection/masterworks/steamboat/index.html> (February 25, 2006).

4. Diane Disney Miller with Pete Martin, "My Dad Walt Disney: Part III," *The Saturday Evening Post*, December 1, 1956, p. 29.

5. Diane Disney Miller with Pete Martin, "My Dad Walt Disney: Part IV," *The Saturday Evening Post*, December 8, 1956, p. 79

6. Katherine and Richard Greene, *The Man Behind the Magic: The Story of Walt Disney* (New York: Viking, 1998), p. 56.

7. Bob Thomas, *Walt Disney: An American Original* (New York: Disney Editions, 1994,) p. 93.

8. "Father Goose," *Time*, p. 45.

9. Frank Nugent, "That Million-Dollar Mouse," *The New York Times Magazine*, September 21, 1947, pp. 22.

10. Ibid., p. 22.

11. "Mr. and Mrs. Disney," *Ladies' Home Journal*, March 1941, p. 20.

12. Christopher Finch, *The Art of Disney: From Mickey Mouse to Magic Kingdoms* (New York: Harry N. Abrams, 1995), p. 66.

13. Katherine and Richard Greene, *Inside the Dream: The Personal Story of Walt Disney* (New York: Roundtable Press, 2001), p. 41.

14. Author interview with Diane Disney Miller, December 9, 2005.

15. Greene, *Inside the Dream: The Personal Story of Walt Disney*, p. 54.

16. Thomas, p. 119.

Chapter 8. All the Colors of the Rainbow

1. Katherine and Richard Greene, *Inside the Dream: The Personal Story of Walt Disney* (New York: Roundtable Press, 2001), p. 43.

2. Muriel Fuller, "Three Little Pigs," *Publishers Weekly*, October 21, 1933, p. 1431.

3. John Scott, "Three Little Pigs and Big, Bad Wolf Clean Up Millions," *Los Angeles Times*, October 8, 1933, pp. A1, 6.

4. Bob Thomas, *Walt Disney: An American Original* (New York: Disney Editions, 1994), p. 119.

5. Ibid., p. 120.

6. "Mr. and Mrs. Disney," *Ladies' Home Journal*, March 1941, p. 146.

7. Amy Boothe Green and Howard E. Green, *Remembering Walt: Favorite Memories of Walt Disney* (New York: Hyperion, 1999), p. 64.

8. "Father Goose," *Time*, December 27, 1954, p. 44.

9. Douglas W. Churchill, "Now Mickey Mouse Enters Art's Temple," *The New York Times Magazine*, June 3, 1934, p. 13.

10. Ibid.

11. Diane Disney Miller with Pete Martin, "My Dad Walt Disney: Part VII," *The Saturday Evening Post*, December 29, 1956, p. 100.

12. Thomas, p. 123.

13. Ibid., p. 126.

14. Diane Disney Miller with Pete Martin, "My Dad Walt Disney: Part V," *The Saturday Evening Post*, December 15, 1956, p. 97.

15. Ibid., p. 98.

16. Frank Nugent, "That Million-Dollar Mouse," *The New York Times Magazine*, September 21, 1947, pp. 22, 60–61.

17. Thomas, p. 128.

18. Walt Disney, "*Snow White and the Seven Dwarfs* Adapted from Grimm's Fairy Tales," *Good Housekeeping*, November 1937, p. 37.

19. Katherine and Richard Greene, *The Man Behind the Magic: The Story of Walt Disney* (New York: Viking, 1998), p. 80.

20. "Walt Disney, 65, Dies on Coast; Founded an Empire on a Mouse," *The New York Times*, December 16, 1966, pp. 1, 40.

21. Greene, *The Man Behind the Magic: The Story of Walt Disney*, p. 80.

22. Thomas, pp.130–131.

23. Frank S. Nugent, "The Music Hall Presents Walt Disney's Delightful Fantasy, 'Snow White and the Seven Dwarfs'—Other New Films at Capitol and Criterion," *The New York Times*, January 14, 1938, p. 21.

24. Author interview with Diane Disney Miller, December 9, 2005.

25. Ibid.

26. Greene, *Inside the Dream: The Personal Story of Walt Disney*, p. 86.

Chapter 9. Fantasy & War

1. Katherine and Richard Greene, *The Man Behind the Magic: The Story of Walt Disney* (New York: Viking, 1998), p. 88.

2. Sam Robins, "Disney Again Tries Trailblazing," *The New York Times Magazine*, November 3, 1940, p. 19.

3. Greene, *The Man Behind the Magic: The Story of Walt Disney*, p. 87.

4. Cathie Labrador, Katherine Greene, Richard Greene, and Walter Elias Disney Miller, producers, and Jean-Pierre Isbouts, director. *Walt: The Man Behind the Myth.* 119 min. Disney Enterprises, Inc., 2004. DVD.

5. Communications with Diane Disney Miller, November 2005 and December 10, 2005.

6. Katherine and Richard *Greene, Inside the Dream: The Personal Story of Walt Disney* (New York: Roundtable Press, 2001), p. 75.

7. Greene, *The Man Behind the Magic: The Story of Walt Disney*, p. 98.

8. "Disney Rides a Baby Elephant Into Hearts of His Fans," *Newsweek*, October 27, 1941, p. 61.

9. Greene, *Inside the Dream: The Personal Story of Walt Disney*, p. 76.

10. "Father Goose," *Time*, December 27, 1954, p. 45.

11. Greene, *The Man Behind the Magic: The Story of Walt Disney*, pp. 100–101.

12. Philip T. Hartung, "Winged Victory [Walt Disney's new film, Victory Through Air Power]," *Commonweal*, August 6, 1943, pp. 393–394.

13. Greene, *Inside the Dream: The Personal Story of Walt Disney*, p. 67.

Chapter 10. "Zip-a-Dee-Doo-Dah!"

1. Amy Boothe Green and Howard E. Green, *Remembering Walt: Favorite Memories of Walt Disney* (New York: Hyperion, 1999), p. 18.

2. Katherine and Richard Greene, *The Man Behind the Magic: The Story of Walt Disney* (New York: Viking, 1998), p. 148.

3. Bill Peet, *Bill Peet: An Autobiography* (Boston: Houghton Mifflin Company, 1989), p. 122.

4. Katherine and Richard Greene, *Inside the Dream: The Personal Story of Walt Disney* (New York: Roundtable Press, 2001), p. 85.

5. Peet, p. 123.

6. Greene, *The Man Behind the Magic: The Story of Walt Disney*, p. 107.

7. Diane Disney Miller with Pete Martin, "My Dad Walt Disney: Part I," *The Saturday Evening Post*, November 17, 1956, p. 133.

8. Green, *Remembering Walt: Favorite Memories of Walt Disney*, p. 19.

9. Ibid, p. 17.

10. Greene, *The Man Behind the Magic: The Story of Walt Disney*, p. 31.

11. Ibid., p. 30.

12. Ibid., p. 33.

13. Greene, *The Man Behind the Magic: The Story of Walt Disney*, p. 109.

14. Ibid., p. 113.

15. Jim Korkis, "Flying High with Walt," August 27, 2003, <http://jimhillmedia.com/mb/columnists/showauthor.php?ID=19> (February 24, 2006).

16. Greene, *The Man Behind the Magic: The Story of Walt Disney*, p. 109.

Chapter 11. The Magic Kingdom

1. Katherine and Richard Greene, *The Man Behind the Magic: The Story of Walt Disney*, (New York: Viking, 1998), p. 109.

2. Valerie J. Nelson, "Fred Joerger, 91; Model Maker, 'Imagineer' for Disneyland Attractions," *Los Angeles Times*, September 5, 2005, p. B9.

3. Greene, *The Man Behind the Magic: The Story of Walt Disney*, p. 123.

4. Ibid., p. 124.

5. Katherine and Richard Greene, *Inside the Dream: The Personal Story of Walt Disney* (New York: Roundtable Press, 2001), p. 95.

6. Amy Boothe Green and Howard E. Green, *Remembering Walt: Favorite Memories of Walt Disney* (New York: Hyperion, 1999), p. 24.

7. Bill Davidson, "The Fantastic Walt Disney," *The Saturday Evening Post*, November 7, 1964, p. 71.

8. Green, p. 48.

Chapter 12. End of an Era

1. Katherine and Richard Greene, *Inside the Dream: The Personal Story of Walt Disney* (New York: Roundtable Press, 2001), p. 117.

2. Katherine and Richard Greene, *The Man Behind the Magic: The Story of Walt Disney* (New York: Viking, 1998), p.143.

3. "Walt Disney, 65, Dies on Coast; Founded an Empire on a Mouse," *The New York Times*, December 16, 1966, p. 40.

4. "Walt's Family and Friends: Dick Van Dyke," The Walt Disney Family Museum, Special Exhibits, Dick Van Dyke, <http:// www. waltdisney.com> (January 2, 2006).

5. Greene, *The Man Behind the Magic: The Story of Walt Disney*, p. 165.

6. Ibid., p. 169.

7. Greene, *Inside the Dream: The Personal Story of Walt Disney*, pp. 177–178.

8. Amy Boothe Green and Howard E. Green, *Remembering Walt: Favorite Memories of Walt Disney* (New York: Hyperion, 1999), p. viii.

9. Jean-Pierre Isbouts, *Discovering Walt: The Magical Life of Walt Disney* (New York: Roundtable Press, 2001), p. 62.

10. Susan Champlin, "Walt's Big Idea," *San Diego Westways Southern California Lifestyle Magazine*, May/June 2005, p. 76.

11. The Walt Disney Family Museum, Special Exhibit Articles, "The Florida Project: An Introduction (Part II)" <http://www.waltdisney.com> (February 24, 2006).

12. Mary McNamara, "Big Man, Huge Home, Tall Tales," *Los Angeles Times*, October 3, 2004, p. E27.

13. Author interview with Diane Disney Miller, December 9, 2005.

FURTHER READING

Gordon, Bruce, and Kevin Rafferty, Randy Webster, David
Mumford. *Walt Disney Imagineering: A Behind the Dream
Look at Making the Magic Real.* New York: Disney
Editions, 1996.

Greene, Katherine and Richard. *Inside the Dream: The
Personal Story of Walt Disney.* New York: Disney Editions,
2001.

Isbouts, Jean-Pierre. *Discovering Walt: The Magical Life of
Walt Disney.* New York: Roundtable Press, 2001.

Nardo, Don. *Walt Disney.* San Diego, Calif.: Lucent Books,
2000.

Schroeder, Russell. *Walt Disney: His Life in Pictures.*
New York: Disney Press, 1996.

Simon, Charnan. *Walt Disney: Creator of Magical Worlds.*
New York: Children's Press, 1999.

INTERNET ADDRESSES

**The Official Web site for the Walt Disney Co.
& Disneyland**
<http://www.Disney.com>

**Family museum with many exhibits, interviews,
activities, biographies, and resources.**
<http://www.waltdisney.com>

A variety of information, photographs, and links.
Note: This Web site has *no* affiliation with the Walt
Disney Co.
<http://www.justdisney.com>

INDEX

Page numbers for photographs are in **boldface** type.

A

Alice cartoon movie series, 48, 50–53, 56–57
Andrews, Julie, 9, 108
animation, 25, 42, 50-51, 61, 73, 82

B

Bambi, 57, 83–84, 90
Bounds, Grace (sister-in-law), 95
Bounds, Hazel (sister-in-law), 52, 79, 87
Bradbury, Ray, 111
Brown, Bob (son-in-law), 106

C

Chaplin, Charlie, **27**, 35
Cinderella, 101

D

Dali, Salvador, 57
Davis, Virginia, 50
Der Fuehrer's Face, 90
Disney Brothers Studio, 51
Disney, Edna Francis (sister-in-law), 44, 55
Disney, Elias (father), 5, 13–15, 18, **19**, 21, 23–25, 28–29, 30, 34, 36, 39, 43, 45, 55, 80, 88
Disney, Flora (mother), 13–14, 17–**19**, 20, 24–25, 29, 30, 36–37, 43, 55, 80, 88
Disney, Herbert (brother), 13, 19, 31, 43–44, 55

Disney, Lillian Bounds (wife), 52–54, 55, 57–59, 62, 67, 69, 72, 77, 79, 87, 95–97, 102–103, 105–106, **107**, 109
Disney, Raymond (brother), 13, 19, 45
Disney, Robert (uncle), 49, 51
Disney, Roy (brother), 13, 16, 19, 21–22, 24, 28, 31, 34, 40, 43, 44, 48, 50-53, 55–57, 61–65, 67, 69–70, 73, 75–77, 79–80, 91, 98, 100, 110–111
Disney, Roy Edward (nephew), 91
Disney, Ruth Flora (sister), 14–17, 22, 25, 27–28, 30, 37, 43, 45, 55, 69, 80, 90, 98
Disney, Sharon Mae (daughter), 77, 94–96, 106, **107**
Disney, Walter Elias, 4, **10**, **12**, 17, **41**, 54, **66**, 71, **82**, **85**, **92**, **94**, **99**, **104**, **107**, 112
  art/cartooning, 21, 23, 29, 39, 50
  born, 13
  died, 110
  early life, 13–14
  education, 17, 22, 26, 30, 33
  farm life, 14–20
  in Chicago, Ill., 13, 14, 19, 30–**33**, 34–35, 43

in Kansas City, Mo.,
21–**23**, 24–29
in Marceline, Mo., 6, 14,
15, 18, 20
lung cancer, 109
married, 55
newspaper route, 21–30
patriotic cartoons, 36, **89**
Red Cross Ambulance
Corps, 36–**37**, 38
Santa Fe Railroad job,
31–**32**
U.S. Post Office job, 34
WED Enterprises, 99
Disneyland television show, 6,
101–102
Disneyland Park, 5–7, 8–9, **10**,
11, 15, 18, **99**, 100–103,
105, 109, 110
Donald Duck, **9**, 74, **76**, 84, 90
Dumbo, 88–89, 93

E
Ellenshaw, Harrison, 102
Ellenshaw, Peter, 102
EPCOT, 108–109, 110, 111

F
Fantasia, 82, 83, 86
Flickinger, Clem, 16–17
Flowers and Trees, 70

G
Goofy, 74, 90
Graham, Don, 73
Grant, Joe, 75, 111
Gurr, Bob, 111

H
Hitler, Adolf, 86, 88, 90

I
The Incredible Journey, 57
Iwerks, Ub, 41–42, 45, 47, 51,
52, 59–64, 67–68, 86–87

J
Jackson, Wilfred, 63
The Jazz Singer, 63
Jiminy Cricket, **82**, 90
Joerger, Fred, 99
Johnston, Ollie, 85
Jolsen, Al, 63

K
Kansas City Film Ad Company,
42, 45
Kimball, Ward, 82, 96
Kroc, Ray, 37

L
Laugh-O-grams, 44–48, 51
Lindbergh, Charles, 61
"Little Red Riding Hood," 45,
46

M
Maas, Russell, 36, 38
Mary Poppins, 9, 108
Mickey Mouse, 5–6, 59–**61**,
62, 64–**66**, 67–70, 74,
76–77, 83, **89**, 90, 106, 109,
110
Mickey Mouse Club, 106
Miller, Diane Disney (daughter), 20, 49, 72, 77, 79, 83,
94, 95, 96, 102, 106, **107**,
109
Miller, Ron (son-in-law), 102,
107
Miller, Walter Elias Disney, 106

Minda, Meyer, 24
Minnie Mouse, 61, 64, 67, 69
Mintz, Charlie, 52, 58, 59
Mouseketeers, 105–106

N
Newman Theater Company, 44

O
The Old Mill, 77
Old Yeller, 57
One Hour in Wonderland, 100
Oswald the Lucky Rabbit,
    57–59
O'Zell Jelly Company, 30, 34,
    39, 43

P
Peet, Bill, 88, 92–93
Pesmen, Louis, 40
Pfeiffer, Walter, 26, 41
Pinocchio, 81–**82**, 86
Plane Crazy, 61–62
Pluto, 74
Powers, Pat, 63–65, 67–68

R
Roosevelt, Franklin Delano, 69,
    89
Rubin, Bill, 40

S
Seal Island, 95
*Snow White and the Seven
    Dwarfs*, 74–76, **78**–79
Silly Symphony, 67, **71**, 77
The Skeleton Dance, 67

Song of the South, **92**–93
Stalling, Carl, 63, 67
Steamboat Willie, 62, 64–65

T
Technicolor, 70
television, 100–102, 106
Thomas, Frank, 96
Three Little Pigs, 71
Treasure Island, 96

V
Van Dyke, Dick, 108
vaudeville, 26, 29, 34, 35, 63
Victory Through Air Power, 90

W
Wald, Jerry, 101
Walt Disney Productions, 6
Walt Disney Studio, 56, 59, 63,
    67, 68, 72, 77, 86, 89, 91,
    101, 106
Walt DisneyWorld Resort, 109,
    110, 111
Winkler, Margaret J., 51, 58
Woods, Ilene, 101
World War I, 33, 37–38
World War II, 86, 88, **89**, 91
World's Fair, 108

Z
Zorro, 106